D0113910

To:

From:

Date:

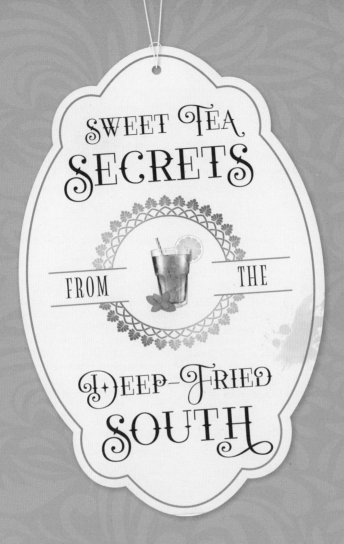

Sweet Tea Secrets from the Deep-Fried South

Jane Jenkins Herlong

Tyndale House Publishers
Carol Stream, Illinois

Living Expressions invites you to explore God's Word in a way that is refreshing to your spirit and restorative to your soul.

Visit Tyndale online at tyndale.com.

Sweet Tea Secrets from the Deep-Fried South: Sassy, Sacred, Southern Stories Filled with Hope and Humor

Designed by Jacqueline L. Nuñez

Edited by Erin Keeley Marshall

ISBN 978-1-4964-5591-8

Printed in China

28 27 26 25 24 23 22
7 6 5 4 3 2 1

In loving memory of my other mother, Ruth Blidgen, who was known on Johns Island as Tootsie. My heart can still hear her beautiful, loving Gullah words, "You know dat Tootsie gwine take good care of her baby. Don' you never fret 'bout nothin."

Contents

Author's Note

MY JAW DROPPED after I hopped on a carriage tour in downtown Charleston. Our guide spoke with a heavy Northern accent, telling me all about Charles Town and the Civil War—but there was nothing civil about that war! (And in the South, we pronounce *war,* wa-wah.) I then spotted a car from Ohio with our sacred South Carolina palmetto tree positioned as the *I* in Ohio. The mutilation of our language and tacky adoption of our precious palmetto tree symbol affixed on the vehicle of an outta-towner was like kudzu winding around my neck. I could barely breathe.

Kudzu (pronounced cud-zoo) is a vine. The South's warmth and humidity provide the perfect conditions for it to grow prolifically, covering everything in its path. Kudzu engulfs buildings and property to the extent that some have called it "the vine that ate the South."

The South has been invaded, rebranded, reprimanded, and ridiculed. We are good folk, but I'm fully aware that some in our midst "need to be furloughed from wince they came." And don't start gaspin' for air like some of our over-the-top church people . . . you know who they are.

I'm going to put this right out there—if you are a born-and-bred Southerner, you will appreciate this book. If you moved here twenty-five years ago and think you are something of a Southern soul, you may chuckle.

If you fled some other part of the Union in hopes of enjoying our lower taxes, lax gun laws, long summer days, and relaxed way of living and talking, you will probably recognize your neighbors in this book. And maybe it will help those of you who aren't from the South to understand us better.

Many of us born-and-bred Southerners hold on to our traditions like we grip MoonPies, which some call pulpwood biscuits. We celebrate Southern-style until the last molecule of dirt is thrown on our face and our family and friends go to the church fellowship hall to talk about how much better we look dead than we ever did alive—all while they are eating potato salad.

I'm fixin' to tell some stories—stories that'll make you cry, tales that'll make you snort until RC Cola rushes from your nostrils. In the South, we never run out of stories. I'm a South Carolinian, and you can't get any more Southern in the South than the southern part of the southeast coast of South Carolina.

My stories will take you through tall coastal marshes that only survive because of the tight grip of pluff mud; so if you feel stuck, keep reading—we have more in common than it may first appear. You will find yourself between the lines of these stories, and although your home may not be my home, you will be reminded of long-lasting life lessons delivered with a Lowcountry Southern perspective.

So come along and laugh with all us Southerners as we attend family reunions that may evolve into dating services. And don't lecture us when we drink our sweet diabetic tea or when we talk about our other favorite beverage . . . gravy. I imagine some of y'all may add extra grease or sugar to your dishes too. Just remember that sugar and grease are not food groups. But some of our old-school Southern cooks may disagree.

If you want to know us, you need to read this book. We are eaten up with secrets, so I decided to do a tell-all Southern humor book. Story is how we speak in the South, so sit in a Charleston rocker, lounge in a Pawleys Island Hammock, or bounce on the joggling board, and enjoy some sweet tea secrets from the deep-fried South.

Introduction

A Southern Lady

Someone who . . .

- Has a pitcher of sweet tea at the ready
- Always writes a thank-you note
- Knows pearls match everything
- Grows her own tomatoes and bakes pies for her neighbors
- Believes in monograms, Mason jars, and mindin' manners
- Is always blessin' someone

When I read the above description to my husband, Thomas, he gave me the yeah-right sarcastic look that only a seasoned Southern husband understands after years of marriage. And, of course, he was correct.

Here's my version:

A Johns Island Southern Woman

Someone who . . .

- Has a pitcher of artificially sweetened tea at the ready with an optional wedge of lemon
- Always writes a thank-you note that does not have the words *thank you* on the front of the note
- Wears pearl earrings but has been told since she was a child that it is not proper for ears to be pierced before age sixteen
- Loves picking vine-ripened tomatoes grown only by her daddy
- Knows that no one will ever be able to make Tootsie's shrimp pie
- Believes in limited use of monograms for clothing, shoes, and purses
- Says "yes, ma'am," and "yes, sir" until the day she dies
- Always refers to her parents as Momma and Daddy

Finally, if you do all of the above, you will be a blessing to your Southern family for generations, if you can keep a secret. 'Cause frankly, my dear, storytelling is our legacy; many in our Southland refer to these tales as . . . *therapy*.

Jane Jenkins Herlong

PART I

THANK DE GOOD LAWD DEY BUILT DE BRIDGE

1
GULLAH, GULLAH JOHNS ISLAND

JOHNS ISLAND is the second largest island on the southern East Coast. For many years, the island was accessible only by boat. My grandfather (Gumpa) always said, "Thank de Good Lawd dey built de bridge" since up till then no one dared marry outside of the family. Actually, we did not have a choice. There was no bridge to get to the other side of the Stono River, so there was no way to infuse new blood into the family. I guess you could say our family tree looked more like one of those wreaths you see in a cemetery that someone forgot to prune.

My family takes pride in being "island people," and our island has its own heartbeat. The pulse of the tides as they ebb and flow . . . the way the coastal breeze exhales as it lifts Spanish moss on gnarled branches . . . the faint buzz of mosquitoes vectoring on your neck and cheek . . . all these sounds remind us that our island is alive.

You won't find much Lowcountry tranquility on the downtown Charleston peninsula. Tourists: that's what you'll find there. Tourists, traffic, rooftop bars, and all the trappings of a city that's almost shed its Southern skin—but not quite. I'll take Charleston over one of those cities north of Richmond any day, but Charleston's not my island.

I grew up playing in old musty homes with large front porches. On lazy Sunday afternoons, I listened to conversations between

Cousin Wee-Wee and Aunt Fannie. Excitement after church was watching airplanes land on the small Johns Island airstrip next to the farm. I learned how to swim when Daddy threw me off the tall dock on Abbapoola Creek. He tossed my siblings and me into the water when the tide was coming in so we could drift down to the metal ladder attached to the floating dock. I crabbed, fished, and went boggin' in the pluff mud on low tide. I adored the Black community—their beautiful style of worship gripped my heart. Jesus was alive and woven into every fiber of their everyday life.

The Gullah language, mostly spoken by the Black community, has deep roots in the Carolina Lowcountry. My grandfather Gumpa spoke this beautiful, almost poetic language fluently. All of us grandchildren loved Gumpa's entertaining storytelling about fishin' in da crik and growin' cukes (cucumbers) in his guar-den.

Back in his day, most people seemed generally thankful to have the island and neighbors who looked out for one another and were kind and loving regardless of gender, skin color, or beliefs. Gumpa often left vegetables from his garden on someone's back doorstep as he sang a song no one recognized . . . just *de de de de*.

We all knew the milkman, and most days we also knew the exact time he exchanged the empty glass bottles for fresh ones of delicious, creamy Coburg milk. Vegetables and fruits magically showed up on your front porch—just 'cause. You see, down a long dirt road, everyone cared for each other. We looked folks in the eye or nodded or waved. Loving your neighbor came natural back then.

As the South of my childhood seemed to shrink, my life experiences and memories grew richer. I value it because we've lost some of its authenticity. I laugh when I recall the unusual events and people across the state who made growing up in rural South Carolina so defining. From the Lowcountry shores of Bird Key Beach to the Upstate and down to the Ridge, I've seen it, loved it, and can't wait to bring it back to life.

My journey begins on Johns Island. How I wish, just one more time, I could breathe in the indescribable scent of my grandmother Lou's biscuits baking while I watched Gumpa tie his jon boat to his dock. God willing, when he takes me to heaven, I'll get to sit a spell on that old floating dock, dangling my legs in that creek one more time, 'cause once upon a time in an old tenant house down a long dirt road lived a little girl with blonde, curly hair and big dreams.

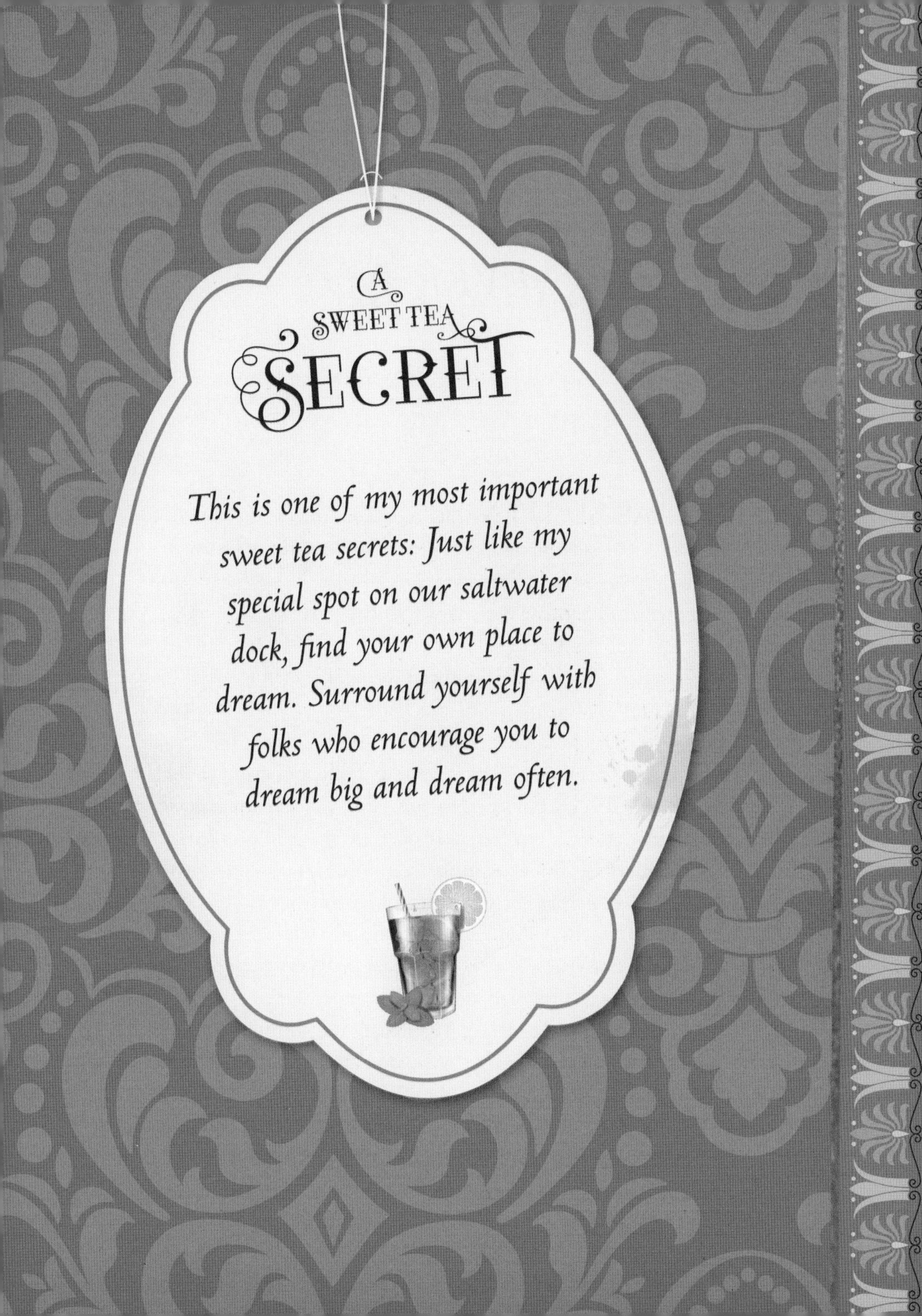
A SWEET TEA SECRET
This is one of my most important sweet tea secrets: Just like my special spot on our saltwater dock, find your own place to dream. Surround yourself with folks who encourage you to dream big and dream often.

2
Never-No

I WAS SIXTEEN years old. Standing on the Charleston Battery, I was surrounded by tourists, locals, and the festive trimmings of three hundred years of history. It was Charleston's tricentennial birthday; the city was in full party mode.

My long hair wrapped around my face as winds from the Ashley River ushered in another Southern spring. I leaned forward on the Battery rail in anticipation of the Tricentennial Boat Parade. And there was that nasty lump in my throat.

The first entry was a massive ship. Folks gathering along the Battery began a chorus of oohs and aahs. Not me; my stomach began to churn.

"Oh, look!" someone in the crowd exclaimed. "There's that gorgeous yacht from the Charleston Marina."

"Well, the next ship will surely win first place," shouted another parade attendee. In all of its glory, that boat was engineered with a fountain of cascading red and blue towers of water.

Then, there was silence. My anxiety was in full throttle. In the midst of the crowd I heard, "Would you look at that!" Ripples of laughter replaced the oohs and aahs.

I did not even have to wonder what caused their reactions. Into the middle of that grand Charleston celebration of yachts and ships floated the *Never-No*—Daddy and Momma's pride and joy. Amid all the elegance and grandeur came our blue-and-white Scottie Craft with the flybridge—all twenty-seven feet of it. Seriously, the *Never-No* looked like a floating matchbox. I wanted to run for cover to hide my embarrassment.

That boat was decorated with every symbol of our state. Yellow jasmine wound up and down the outriggers. A massive blue-and-white South Carolina flag, almost as large as the boat itself, flew proudly over the stern. Bringing up the stern was a palmetto tree with a stuffed, homemade Carolina wren resting in its palms.

But the kicker? The crew—as rough and rowdy as they come. They were having the time of their lives.

"Lawd have mercy, those people sho know how to have fun. They don't care about the size of dat boat," remarked a woman in her Gullah brogue.

My heart swelled. I turned to the woman who made that comment and said, "Thank you! That's my momma and daddy." That dear woman understood—my family, my island, and my upbringing.

I will never forget that moment. It is frozen in time as I watched my parents and their best buds enjoy their own private party on the *Never-No*. My parents knew how to make the most of what they had. That moment represented years of hard work by a handful of Johns Island tomato farmers who toiled in the unforgiving Lowcountry heat to celebrate their field of dreams. I also realized that some out there will always throw tomatoes at your field of dreams.

I remember the evening when the Johns Island farmers gathered around the old yellow Formica table in our small kitchen to name the new boat. It was the Yalta Conference to this gang of tightly woven island friends.

After several names were thrown into the mix, my mother chimed in. "Let's call it the *Never-No*. You never know when you are going, you never know what will happen, and you never know when you are coming home."

It was the pull of the tide and the mounds of hidden pluff mud that my mother was referring to. Momma was spot-on. Life is filled with uncontrollable tides and hidden sandbars of uncertainty.

Today, as I see that old boat now parked in my nephew's yard, I remember all of the fun times, hard work, and many changes. Just like the name of our boat, life is loaded with "never-no" moments that challenge our character and test our future. I do know one thing for sure: If you love God and love yourself, you will know how to love others.

Memories of the *Never-No,* watching my parents and their friends celebrate, and hearing that simple comment from a bystander began to open my eyes to the gift of being reared a "Johns Island girl." I realized that my life was a kaleidoscope of both nature and nurture. What a gift to be surrounded by some of the greatest teachers who made me proud of heritage and taught me that all folks are God's special handiwork.

Maybe sharing that story gave me the courage to tell the next story . . . and the next.

As I type this story, I look to my right and see a prized possession hanging on the wall. A plaque engraved and adorned with gold commemorative tricentennial coins reads:

CHARLESTON TRICENTENNIAL

FIRST PRIZE BOAT PARADE

BEST TRICENTENNIAL THEME

NEVER-NO

BENJAMIN R. JENKINS

APRIL 12, 1970

It was not the size of the boat in the parade but the hearts and passion of those involved. Ya know, just like the name of my parents' boat . . . you just *Never-No.*

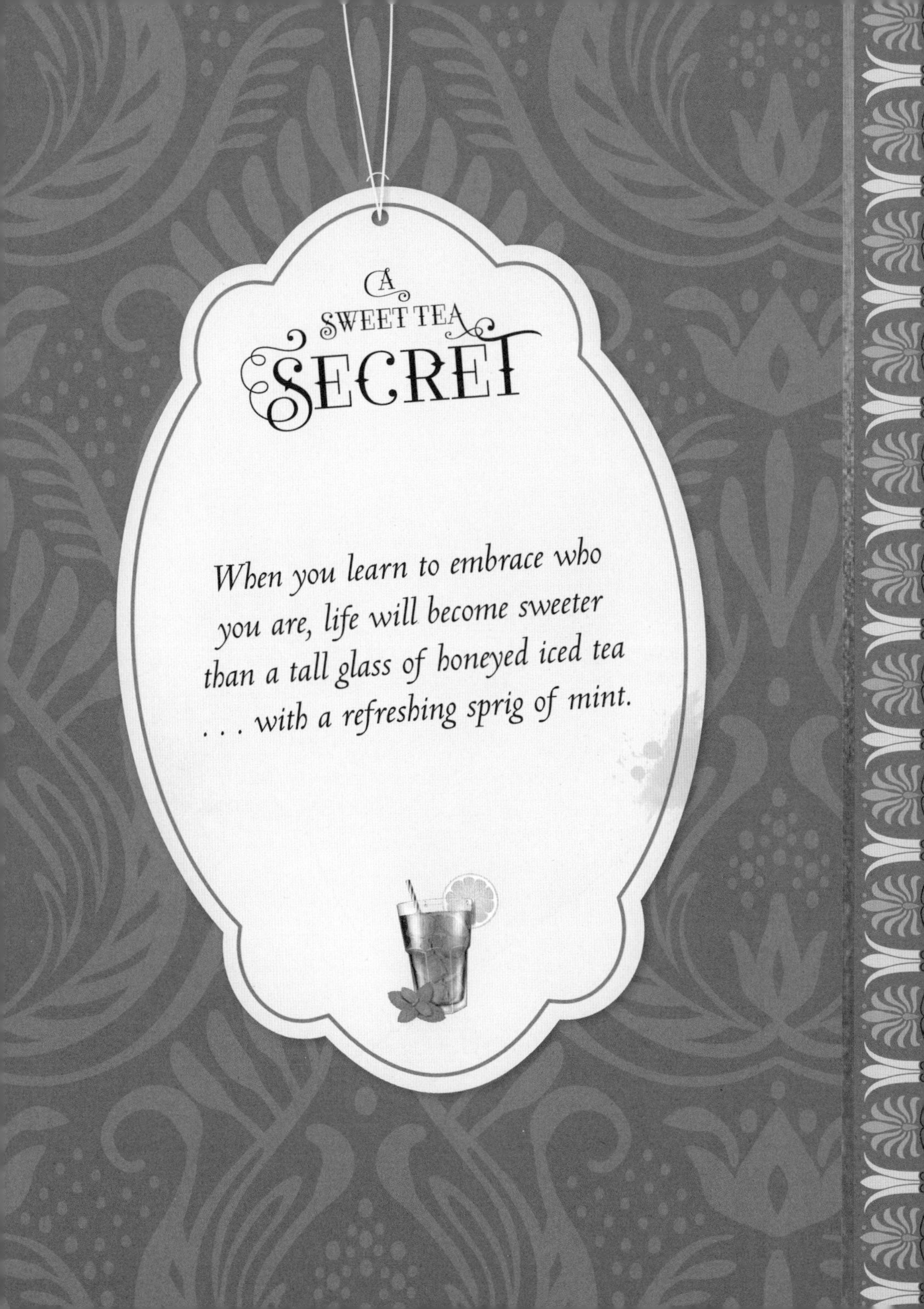

A SWEET TEA SECRET

When you learn to embrace who you are, life will become sweeter than a tall glass of honeyed iced tea . . . with a refreshing sprig of mint.

PART II

My Favorite Brethern and Sistern

3

THE TIE THAT BINDS . . . OUR HEARTS

I LOVED 9:00 A.M. on the farm. I would drive down our long dirt road to pick up Tootsie. Her birth name was Ruth Blidgen, but her "cradle name" was Tootsie. I was only five months old when she came into our lives.

As Tootsie and I drove back to the house, we passed folks on the farm who had been working since sunrise alongside my father in the fields. Some were clearing ditches, others riding on the back of a planter or driving Daddy's John Deere tractors cutting through fresh dirt preparing the land. All were working together, organizing the farm for spring planting. My favorite farm scent to this day is fresh dirt being turned over by plows. It was a team effort that created jobs, grew fresh vegetables, and created memories of Johns Island agriculture. Sadly, much of that environment has been replaced by large housing subdivisions—except on The Hut.

The Hut is a beautiful historic piece of property Daddy bought back in 1961. Forty four-hundred-year-old majestic live oaks spread their massive limbs across the land, resembling giant arms hugging memories from the past. If only those trees could talk—oh, what glorious tales would be told. The land is nestled on Hut Creek, whose flowing tides are continually filled with rich sea life from the Intracoastal Waterway. This was ground zero for our farm.

I remember seeing Daddy jump into his pickup after one of his workers, James, had used it to drive around the farm. James's hearing was impaired, and when Daddy cranked up his truck, the sudden blare of music was earsplitting. I will never forget the look on Daddy's face. After he calmed down and got his hearing back, Momma made an appointment to arrange for James to be fitted with hearing aids.

When the doctor asked James if he knew what had happened to his hearing, James chuckled while telling the doctor that his brother said a cockroach had laid eggs in his eardrum. "Thank dah Lawd, Mrs. Jenkin done brung me down yuh to see you. My brother say he gwine spray some of dat Hot Shot in my ear!"

This is just one of many stories of how much Daddy loved and cherished all of this team; he wanted to make sure everyone was taken care of, even James and the cockroach eggs.

When the *Never-No* pulled into the dock on Abbapoola Creek after a day of deep-sea fishing, countless folks were invited to help themselves to dolphin (not Flipper), red snapper, and other deep-sea delicacies. Bags of cabbage and crates of tomatoes and corn were given away. Daddy knew exactly what he was doing. Some of the island's finest cooks would create amazing Southern dishes and bring them to our home.

Welcome to life on our Lowcountry farm.

I ugly-cried when I watched *The Help*. The life depicted in that movie was nothing like the way we lived on our Johns Island farm. We loved and respected the local community, and the feeling was mutual. My daddy would have never been a successful farmer without his team: Alonzo, Lab, Spike, James, Tootsie, Conchie, Robbie, Mena, Roseanne, and many others. These folks were our extended family.

I remember one time when Daddy came into the house for midday dinner crying and sniffling. "Alonzo has diabetes," he said as he buried his head in his worn, calloused hands.

Then the next week he told one of the funniest stories I've ever heard. Chuckling all the way to the table, Daddy said, "Boy, Lab sure put a cussin' on me today! He said, 'Mr. Benjamin, when you shet yo' eye fo the last time,

I gwine tell dem peoples to bury you under eight feet deep! Dat way, when Gabriel blow his horn, you be the last one up!'"

Another story Daddy told was about taking our male cat to the veterinarian to be neutered. Daddy asked Conchie to hold the cat in his lap while Daddy drove. All the way to the veterinarian's office, Daddy heard Conchie lamenting, "Good Lawd, kitt'nee, I sho glad I ain't you."

We slapped our knees when laughing and wiped our eyes when shedding tears of sorrow. You cannot put a price on those many moments filled with humor, hard work, and "heart" work. Next you'll meet the rest of our family.

I thank God I was taught to love others and appreciate different ways of living. Embracing others yields a sweet tea experience like no other.

4

Roseanne

She was part of our extended family before my time, but I was told that Roseanne smoked a pipe filled with rabbit tobacco, always tied her hair in a scarf, and had one gold tooth. When she smiled, it was literally a golden moment.

Roseanne worked for us when Momma was expecting my oldest sibling, Benny. When Momma began to have horrible labor pains, Roseanne, in her old-school way, said, "Miss Eleanor, go quick an git me dah hatchet and uh bobby pin! Den go lie down on duh bed! I gwine put dat hatchet un'neath duh bed so it can cut duh pain! An dat bobby pin gonna hold duh pain till that baby bon!"

Momma told me that when you're hurting, you'll try just about anything.

After Benny was born, Roseanne cared for him like he was her own. One day, Momma watched Roseanne read a book to my toddler brother. She was quite animated and read flawlessly. Momma peeked over Roseanne's shoulder. On closer inspection, Momma realized as Roseanne "read" from the Little Golden Book, she was making up the story from the pictures. My brother sat on her lap, captivated by every word. Just because Roseanne could not read did not mean she could not tell a story. She made use of her imagination and was an amazing storyteller. In her late eighties, Roseanne decided to attend adult literacy classes, where she learned how to read and write.

Roseanne thought of clever ways to make my brother finish his meals. As a young child, Benny loved playing outside more than he cared about food. Roseanne placed him sitting at the top of our staircase, and every time he took a bite of food, he was allowed to move down one step closer to the door leading outside.

When I was a child, Roseanne fascinated me. She was known for being kindhearted, hardworking, and always a teacher. She was also a caregiver who sacrificed attending school to take care of her siblings.

I remember her as the woman with the golden tooth and shining smile, who "read" Little Golden Books. But mostly she had a 24-carat attitude.

We see so many who allow their limitations to stifle them, and then there are those who are empowered to find another way to accomplish their goals.

5 WILHELMINA

WE CALLED HER MENA. She was a large, loving woman. Daddy built Mena and her husband, Ben, a small home at the mouth of our road. I visited her on Saturdays and watched her dust her knickknacks as soulful gospel music blared through her home. Her heartfelt love of Jesus shone through the way her unwavering faith helped her handle the trials of being a mother of five, two of whom died in a house fire. I was in awe of her new wigs and impressive church-lady finery. Mena also knew how to recycle before *recycling* became a household word. When she babysat us, Mena washed the paper plates and lined them up to dry. Not all fine china is expensive.

One Saturday morning, we heard gunshots. We just knew something was terribly wrong. Daddy hopped into his yellow pickup and took off down the road to find out what had happened. It seemed like forever before the long trail of dust settled. We waited for what seemed to be hours: Momma, my sister, and me crying, holding on to each other, praying for Mena and her family. Finally, Daddy drove up with the news that Ben had gotten drunk and shot Mena. Thank God it was a flesh wound, and she was not terribly hurt, but after that incident, Mena did the unthinkable—she divorced Ben.

Our world changed and our hearts were heavy when Mena started a new life in Newark, New Jersey. Such a thing wasn't normally done in the Johns Island community. Although we knew it was best for her, one of our precious family members was moving away. We missed seeing her laugh with her whole body but mostly we missed her loving heart. Every summer we made sure to visit her when she came back to visit her Johns Island home.

Mena was a brave, caring, fun-loving woman who took all the abuse she could, then took care of herself. Long before #MeToo, there was Mena—a woman far ahead of her time. What a blessing to have lived in the shadow of such an incredibly courageous woman. I pray she found the peace she deserved.

A
SWEET TEA
SECRET
Some of the South's finest treasures
lie at the end of a long dirt road.

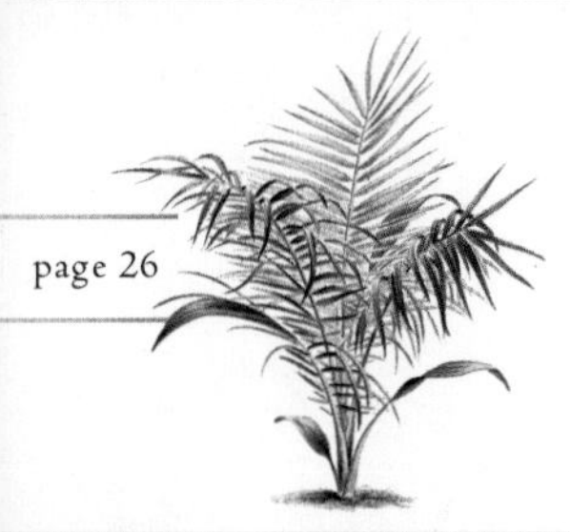

6

Robbie

ROBERT FIELDS'S farm was directly across from the iconic Moving Star Hall, but on Johns Island Robert Fields himself was a moving star. Momma said practically every morning at 5:00 a.m., she awoke to the sounds of hoes cutting the dirt in the field next to her window. Robbie's children were required to manicure the rows before school and then again after school. Robbie and his wife, Nancy, reared a family of nine. Here are the first eight: Anna, Fredrick, Robert Junior (Tunk), Joseph, Juanita, Philip (Cherry Man), Dot, and Dan. Dot was a boy and Dan was a girl. On Johns Island, we like to mix things up with both cradle names and gender names that really don't matter. Number nine is Abraham, or Tootie (not to be confused with Tootsie). Due to a medical error treating a severe ear infection, Tootie lost his hearing but that didn't prevent him from getting a driver's license. For years, his license plate read: HEAR ME.

No doubt about it, the Fields family is still being heard today. Their hard work has reaped success: They are nationally recognized organic farmers who run a lucrative operation. Robbie knew hard work paid and paid well if you kept at it.

The day Robbie passed away Tootsie asked me to go with her to the church to view the body. Robbie and Tootsie were related and she always put her family first. Knowing how superstitious Tootsie could be, I thought someone should take her there. We walked into the empty church, which was filled with flowers and blue ribbons, Robbie's favorite color.

About the time Tootsie and I leaned over the casket, the smoke-alarm battery burped, indicating a low battery. Tootsie screamed, jumped, and grabbed my waist since she was not much taller than my chest. She scared me so badly I grabbed her head.

In the middle of all this, we both hit the casket, and in horror I watched Robbie's lifeless body rock back and forth. Tootsie exclaimed, "Do Lawd, Robbie! Don' you git up out dat casket! Jedus done call you home!"

Eventually Robbie settled back in his box, as we all will one day. It took Tootsie and me a lot longer to settle. Robbie Fields was the type to keep going even after death. America could use more men like Robbie Fields.

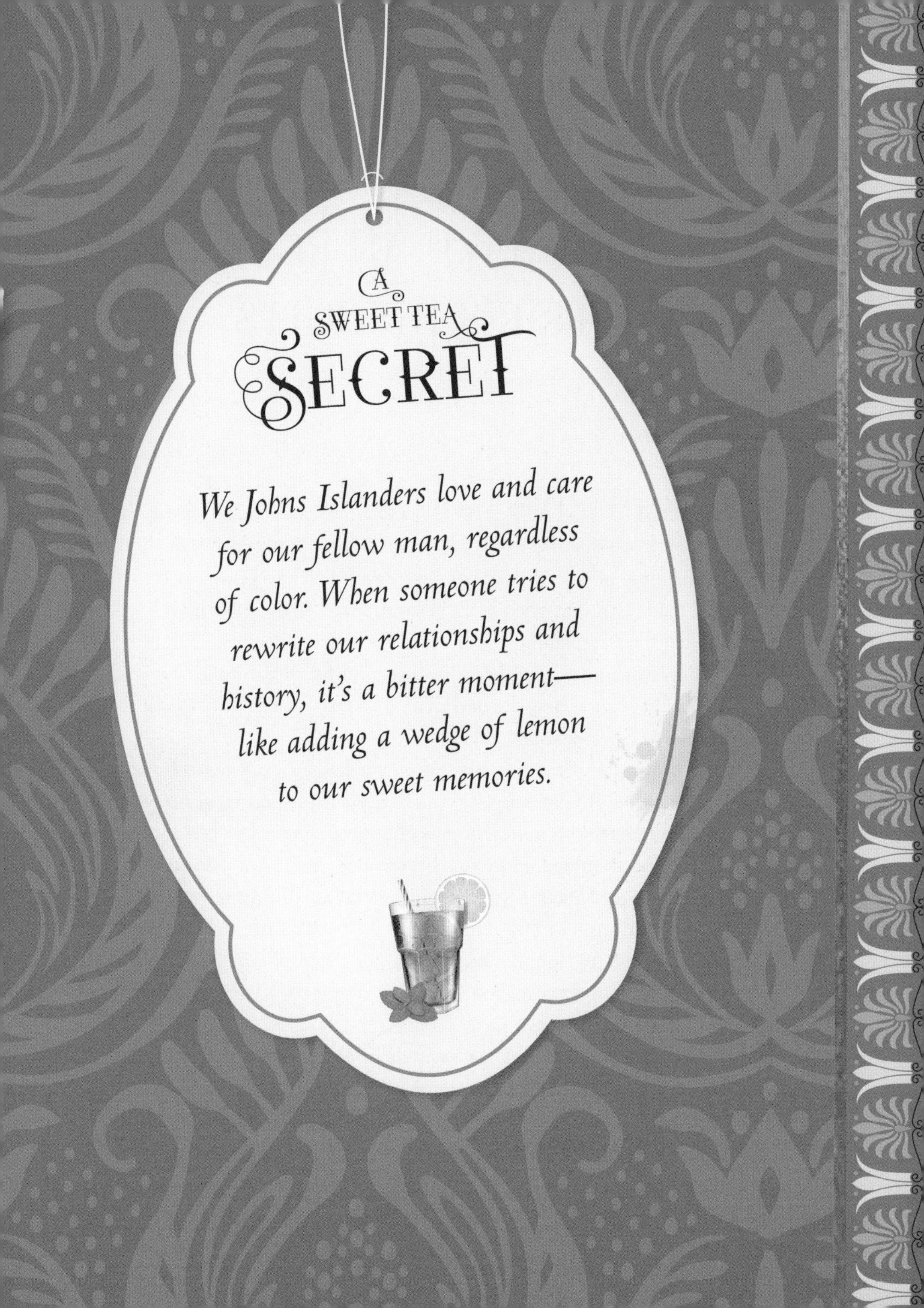
A SWEET TEA SECRET
We Johns Islanders love and care for our fellow man, regardless of color. When someone tries to rewrite our relationships and history, it's a bitter moment—like adding a wedge of lemon to our sweet memories.

7

"Lord-Have-Mercy," Tootsie's Biscuits

RUMMAGING AROUND in my momma's kitchen pantry, I could always spot the old green tin container. It was always in the same place and contained whatever delicious treasures Tootsie had made that day. She knew the container was the first thing I looked for after a long school day. Tootsie had already gone home, but not without leaving her signature treat for me to find. You see, I was "baby girl," and she never failed to tell others, "I dun raise she sence she ben five-munt old."

Years later, I sat cross-legged on the beige vinyl kitchen floor, holding that old green tin. I thought about Tootsie and how she filled that container with delicacies few could replicate. How blessed I was to have been influenced by this beautiful woman who worked with my family for almost fifty years. Her rich Gullah culture was laced with traditions, customs, and cuisine that stuck with me more than a Charleston Rice Spoon mouthful of her steaming-hot grits. Not only was Tootsie an amazing cook, she was a loyal friend and beautiful soul—a Southern treasure.

When I was a child, the excitement of opening the top of that green tin was a ritual that spanned many years. It held its own unique thrill, like Christmas Day, the first day of school, or my thirteenth birthday. There was always a surprise inside the tin. But whatever the treat, one thing was sure: Love and respect were always baked into every bite.

On the farm, Momma and Tootsie made sure that the midday meal was hearty enough to energize Daddy for the remainder of his workday. Big meals were a challenge, especially during tomato season when we entertained Daddy's tomato brokers from as far away as central Florida. But no restaurant specialty could compare with Tootsie's Lowcountry soul food. Sometimes guests left money on the windowsill in appreciation for her hard work. Tootsie loved those crisp twenty-dollar bills.

Some days the green container was filled with Tootsie's fried chicken. Her secret-recipe batter was loaded with spices that made your taste buds explode. Or maybe there'd be a bowl of fresh "vege-tables" from the "guar-den," as Tootsie said. A slice of her shrimp pie was another treasure I sometimes found in the tin. No doubt, the finest chefs in Charleston would have paid a pile of money to have her signature shrimp pie on their menus. My absolute favorite find, though, was when Tootsie used her famous biscuit recipe to decorate the top of her many other Lowcountry dishes.

No way could I, or Momma either, ever make biscuits like Tootsie's. And believe me, I tried. I followed her recipe to the letter: same kneading technique and same old charred baking pan. When my biscuits came out of the oven, I could not wait for those flaky layers to melt in my mouth. Instead, I bit into a brick of dough heavy as a rock.

Tootsie stood right beside me that day. Her contagious laughter rang through the kitchen. "Do Lawd, these gwine break yo teeth!"

Tootsie and I had countless flour fights in our farmhouse kitchen, and many times we laughed so hard we ended up on the floor wrapped in each other's arms. (You can see the evidence in the photo on page 16.) Maybe it's best that I never mastered making her biscuits. Some Southern dishes are so sacred, they just need to be honored with remembrance. Tootsie's culinary craftsmanship was like the work of a great artist—never meant to be duplicated, just admired.

On rare days I opened the lid of that container hoping to find half a biscuit or even a crumb, but to my great sorrow, the container was empty. I had to settle for Sister Schubert's or "whop biscuits." (For those who don't know about "whop biscuits," think of the sound made when you peel the wrapper and hit the kitchen counter with that cylinder filled with dough. It makes a "whop" sound.)

During my childhood, I could smell Tootsie's prized, oddly shaped biscuits as soon as I entered the back hall of our home. Tootsie knew exactly what I wanted . . . our little secret. "Come yuh, Baby. You know dat Tootsie neva gwine forget 'bout doin' for her Dupe." I loved it when she called me her pet name. Those words comforted me like a blanket on a winter night.

As I entered the kitchen, the aroma made my mouth water. Piled high on a plate, delicious and golden brown, Tootsie's biscuits sat on the counter. And there, on top of the stack, the other prize: the baby biscuit. "I done fix you yo' a baby biscuit," Tootsie said in her poetic, loving voice.

I could always count on her to bake a bite-size morsel just for me . . . the last child born to Eleanor and Benjamin Jenkins . . . the five-month-old child she diapered when she came to work for the first time.

Tootsie was my *I Love Lucy* pal . . . the only woman who could fake crying and make me stay at home with her instead of going with Momma to Sam Solomon to buy the Mickey Mouse talking telephone I coveted for years. We created tents out of sheets on the clothesline and made mud pies on the back steps of our old farmhouse. This is the woman I taught how to drive Daddy's truck, narrowly missing the ditch. She cried with me when my daddy died and held me in her strong black arms when Momma was sick.

Tootsie was my hero. She gave years of love, care, and dedicated service to my family. She protected me from spankings I deserved, reprimands I should have received, and sicknesses that only her remedies could cure. Her home-brewed medicinal concoctions were "tea and tose" with a swig of ginger ale or a dash of baking soda. She could do anything—even transform a leftover ball of dough into a gift of love that made me feel cherished. I miss her one-of-a-kind culinary creations, but most of all I miss her. She, too, was one of a kind.

Blessed are those of us who have loving, nurturing folks in our lives like Tootsie. Whatever their shape, size, or color, they make us feel warm and secure.

On a still night, when I am sitting under the Johns Island live oak trees by the banks of Hut Creek, Tootsie's Gullah voice drifts on the salty wind that whispers through the tall coastal marsh, "Come yuh, Baby. You know dat Tootsie gwine take good care of her baby. Don' you never fret 'bout nothin."

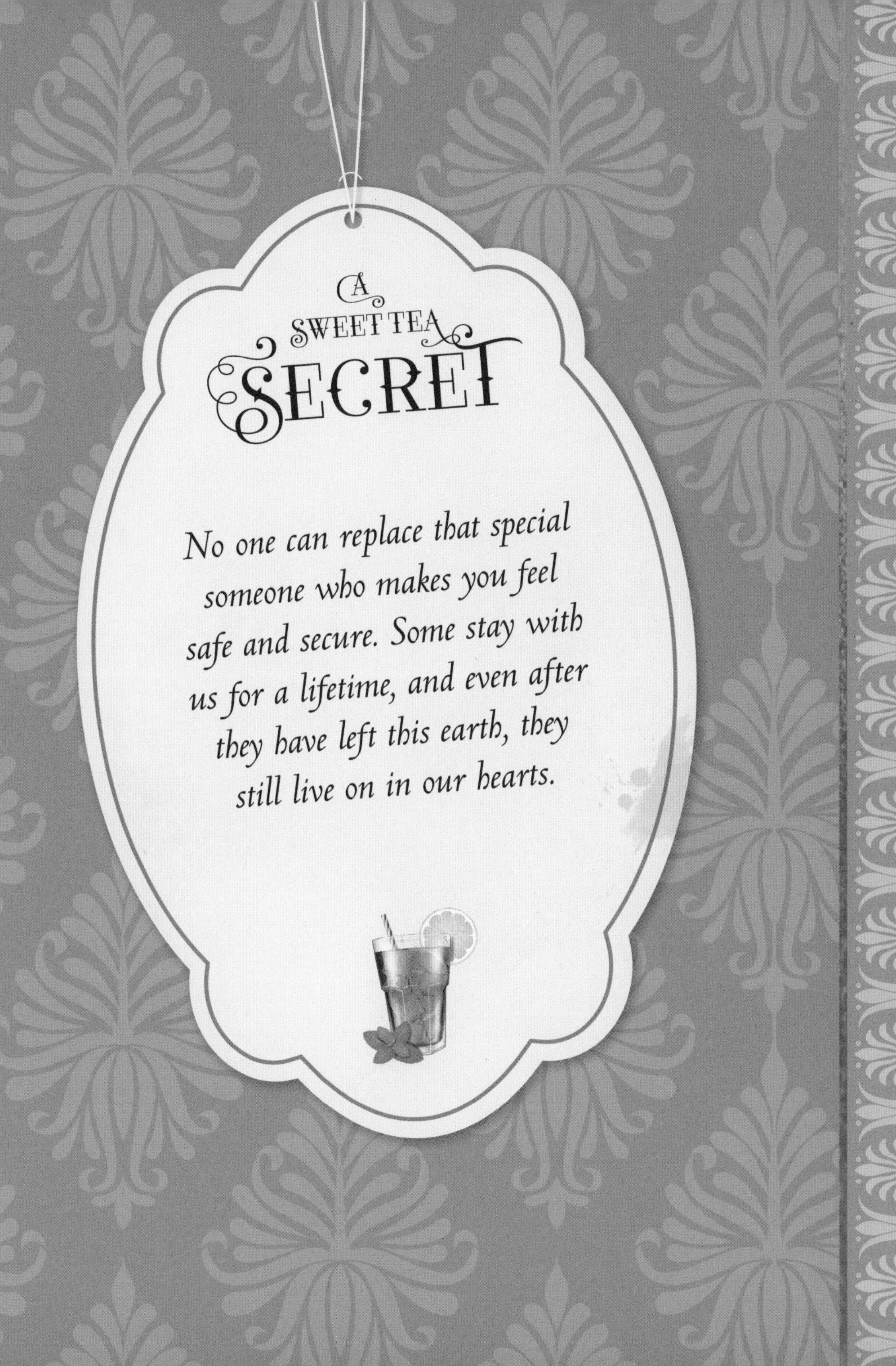

A Sweet Tea Secret

No one can replace that special someone who makes you feel safe and secure. Some stay with us for a lifetime, and even after they have left this earth, they still live on in our hearts.

PART III

Keeping the Faith

8
THE CHURCH OF *SOUTHERN* ENGLAND

DURING MY CHILDHOOD, I slowly learned the ways of being an Episcopalian. One of *the* "rules" of the Episcopal Church required confirmed women to cover their heads. I had to wear a lacy round thing on my head that was attached by a bobby pin. I often forgot to bring the scrap of lace with me to church, and half the time lost its little plastic holder. One super-religious woman, who sat on the other side of the church, forgot her headwear too. She was so determined to be covered that, in desperation, she wore a paper napkin on her head.

Frankly, I thought being an Episcopalian was boring until I was old enough to understand the *Book of Common Prayer*. Knowing when to kneel, sit, stand, and sing is still a challenge. My faith walk has been stretched to the max since I have traveled around the denominational block. I went to a Baptist high school, attended a Methodist college, and almost married a Roman Catholic. After Thomas and I married, I joined the small Methodist country church where he was a member. Three-fourths of the folks in its cemetery are Herlongs.

If you're an Episcopalian, I know what you are thinking: *She dated a Roman Catholic*? But in my defense, he was a hottie astronaut. Okay, let me be totally honest: He was a Roman Catholic Yankee. But did I mention that he was a hottie astronaut?

When my romance with the hottie was in full-throttle, out-of-this-world, on-cloud-nine, seeing-stars mode, I went to my cousin's wedding. Momma warned me *not* to tell my childhood minister (who happened to be officiating the ceremony) under any circumstances that I was dating a Roman Catholic. That sort of romance was frowned upon since a good Southern Episcopalian must marry her own kind. Even marrying a Methodist was questionable.

But my secret was exposed at the reception when our dear Episcopal minister asked, "So, Jane, are you dating anybody?"

Momma cut her eyes at me. I knew that look. She was saying, "Lie to this man of God."

But my mind raced to the pearly gates and to what St. Peter might say to me if I did lie: "Well, we *would* have let you in but you lied to the man of God who baptized and confirmed you, so—"

I told the truth. "Yes, sir. I am dating someone." (I thought it best not to mention that he was a hottie astronaut.)

"Is he a member of our denomination?"

"Um . . . no, sir. He is actually Roman Catholic."

Our dear Episcopal minister's face cracked like the concrete St. Peter statue in the church's prayer garden. Turned that color, too. His normal pinkish-tawny cheeks changed to a shade of ashy gray. The small, clear glass plate he held hit the tiled floor and shattered. The levity of the moment ceased; all eyes looked our way. A cherry tomato rolled across the floor of the church fellowship hall. Not only did the tiny cherry tomato roll, the minister's eyes rolled too.

I'm telling the truth, so help me St. Peter.

At that moment, I left the church of my childhood. When I stepped outside of the Church of Southern England, I discovered a whole new worship experience called the Southern Tent Revival.

Sometimes you find church. Sometimes church finds you. Occasionally, God uses a hottie astronaut to lead you closer to him.

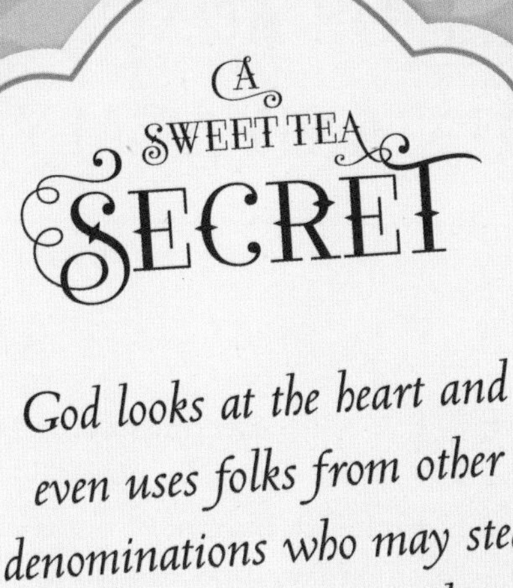

God looks at the heart and even uses folks from other denominations who may steal your heart. The bottom line is to have a closer walk with the one who sees you and desires a relationship over our religion.

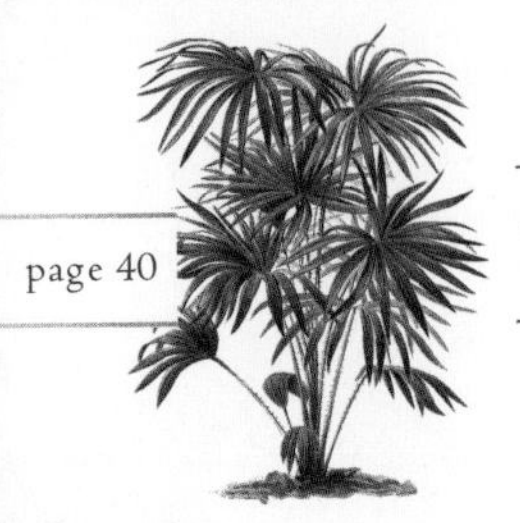

9
REVIVE US AGAIN AND AGAIN AND AGAIN

I LOST COUNT of how many times I accepted Jesus as my Savior.

When I was a teenager, I knelt in front of our television when Billy Graham gave his salvation invitation. His words were so convicting, so full of truth, and so full of warning about what would happen if I refused to give my life to Christ that I was afraid I would spend eternity stuck in pluff mud on low tide with a million fiddler crabs pinching me. In the South, there is no such thing as being prayed up too much.

I'm sure Jesus smiled at my many attempts to make sure I would go to heaven when I died. But in case you're wondering, Lord, you had me at the last verse of "I Surrender All," page 162.

There are so many interpretations on how to get to heaven. Some Baptists say, "Once saved, always saved." Others disagree. But I say, "Thank God, I'm not God."

No Southern worship experience compares to a good old-fashioned tent revival preached by a good old-fashioned Southern preacher. It moves the heart. Moves souls to dig in their pockets and purses and give deep. Moves the big-bosomed wives of the gospel singers to turn their fancy rings around so the ushers can't see the flashy gems. I sang at a tent revival with a famous gospel group and

when the offering plate was passed around . . . well, let's just say I know of what I preach.

Late one evening, a revival regular approached the minister and said, "Preacher, the crowd is not as big tonight. I bet it's 'cause of all them snakes last night."

"Snakes?" asked the pastor.

"Yes, snakes. Some folks who came last night said there were snakes all over the place."

"It's not the snakes," said the preacher. "Don't you know that is the devil trying to keep you and them away?"

After their conversation, I commented to the preacher, "Gracious! The lies some people tell to try to ruin this tent revival."

"Oh, there are snakes everywhere," the minister confessed. "Saw them myself under chairs and such. I suspect the vibration from the music is making them slither from the woods."

I've heard of preachers handling snakes, but it never occurred to me that maybe snakes need saving too. If you believe the Bible (which I do), Satan was a snake. Maybe some in the crowd that night were his kin. Regardless, after that evening, my walk with the Lord improved. By that I mean I watched more closely where I walked during the tent revival.

Not long after the snake episode, Thomas and I were invited to sing at an outdoor revival in the foothills of rural Georgia. The minister made the Gospel Sing setting sound lovely, but this event was held in an asphalt parking lot between two tall buildings . . . in August. I wore a cute sundress and sat in a Masters golf tournament chair. Chocolate pudding on a white Easter dress would have blended in better.

Another singing group performed too. They pulled up to the revival in a late-model, powder-blue bus that was the color of a packet of a certain artificial sweetener. One by one, they filed out of the bus—all wearing homemade outfits the same color as the bus. The family obeyed strict rules of their denomination, and some in that faith believe women should not cut their hair. So the younger women had shorter hair swept into updos; the older ladies had longer hair, which was piled higher. That last woman off the bus had a hairstyle that rivaled Marge Simpson's. Seriously, she had to duck her head to get off of the bus.

I remember exactly what we sang that evening because it is one of only two songs Thomas can sing without messing up the words. After we sang "We Have This Moment," I was asked to introduce the other gospel group, led by Marge Simpson. "Please welcome our next group, who will share more about God's amazing love, grace, and forgiveness," I said in a sweet tone.

"Thank ya, Sister Herlong," said the woman with the highest hairdo. "Friends, we gon sing, 'God Is Gonna Git Cha If You Don't Do Right.'"

As polished and professional as I thought Thomas and I were, this group ministered with a lot more heart, soul, and moisture than we did. (And believe me, I'd poured out pints.) The folks in attendance just loved them.

It was a sweet tea Southern revelation revival moment for me: God looks at a person's heart. He doesn't care about way-too-big hair, dresses that match buses, or cute sundresses worn by folks sitting in Masters golf tournament chairs. What matters is how we act before the Master.

A
SWEET TEA
SECRET
Sometimes it's not the performance that matters but the Person for whom you are performing.

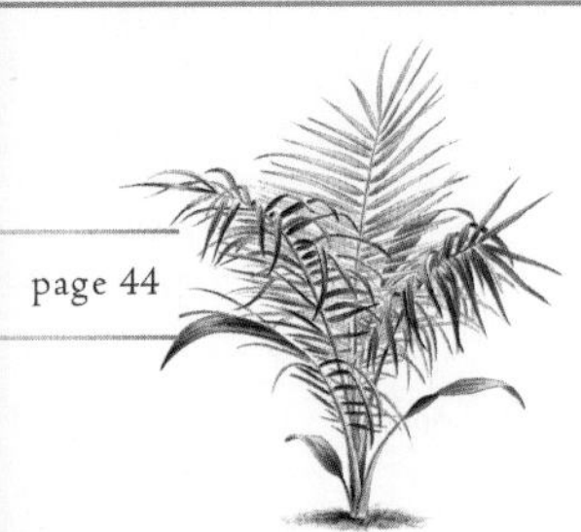

10

SOUTHERN ALTAR CALLS

IN THE SOUTH, a church service usually concludes with an altar call. And the traditional song we sing is "Just As I Am." Now I love that song, and all six of its verses. But some preachers will get into "the flesh," as we say in the South, and they panic when no one is heading down to the altar by the end of verse five.

I've heard preachers say, "Now I know there are some of you who need the Lord, and I feel him calling you to come down." Then verse six cranks up, and to the embarrassment/offense of the preacher, no one makes their way to the front. When that happens, some relentless preachers give it another go.

"Okay, we will hum the song . . ."

"All right, now," the preacher would say, "we will pray as we listen to the music . . ." And here came the zinger line that tested my faith more than anything, "With every head bowed and every eye closed, confess your sins," said the preacher/evangelist. "No one will look, just come to the altar with all of your horrible sins." Most of the time, I cracked my eye open just to see these terrible people. It's like seeing a note taped to the side of a building: Wet Paint.

Still no takers.

Y'all think I'm kidding, but I've been there. Some of you have too. And when this happens, when we're called to beseech the Lord,

I find myself praying for someone to make the trip down to the altar and confess their sin so we can eat the covered-dish casseroles.

There are altar calls and the call of God, but sometimes the most powerful call of all is the call of nature. And I can testify that when nature calls, some brave soul will walk to the front and reconfess an already confessed confession. Seriously, who are we trying to impress? The Lord already knows all of our faults and needs. He knows what's in our hearts and loves you and me anyway. Just like the song title says, "Just As I Am."

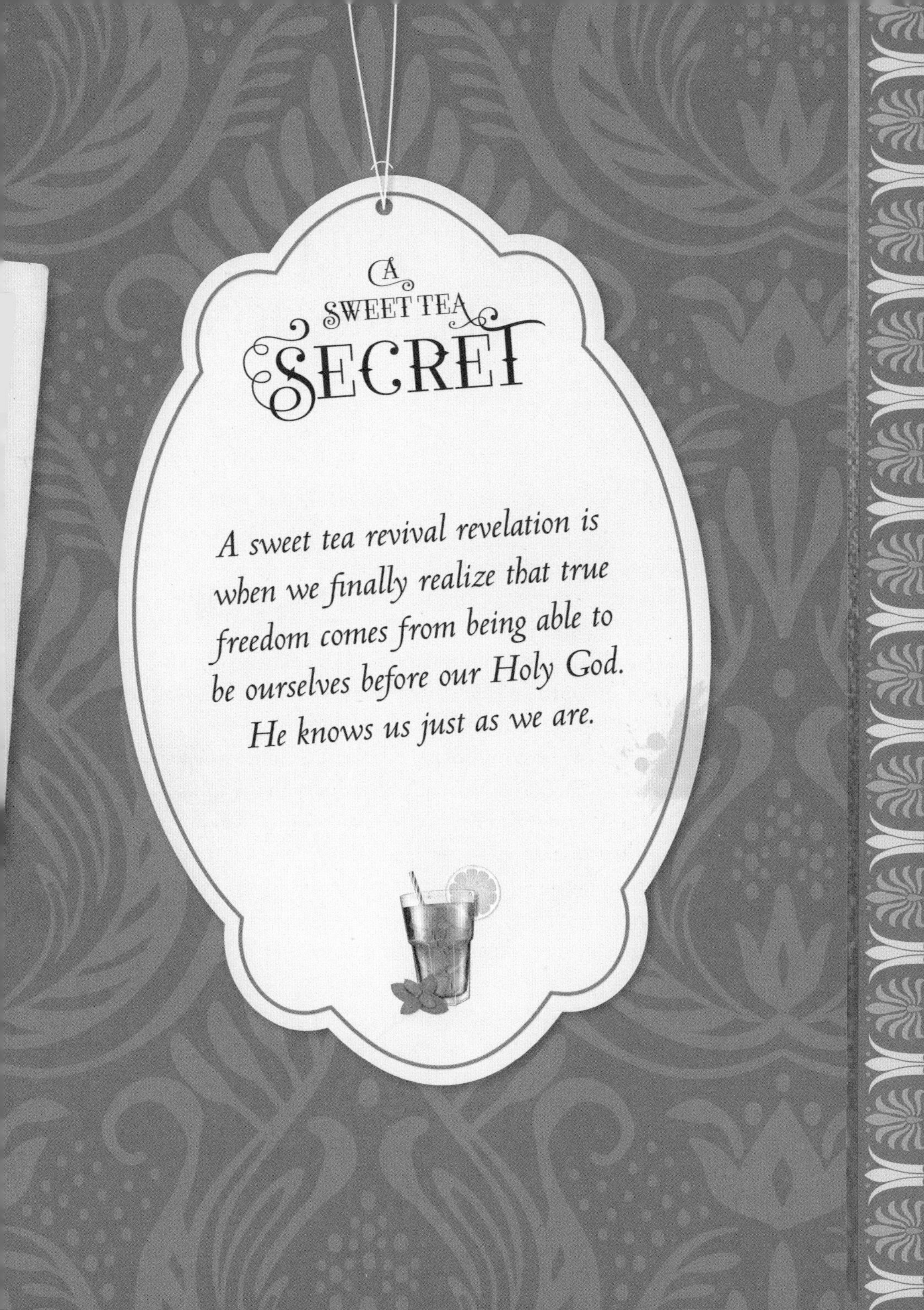
A
SWEET TEA
SECRET
A sweet tea revival revelation is when we finally realize that true freedom comes from being able to be ourselves before our Holy God. He knows us just as we are.

11

OW-AH SACRED, DEEP-FRIED CHURCH CELEBRATIONS

"JA-UN, get out of the kitchen," said my mother with true Old Testament conviction. "Believe me," she continued, "your time will come to learn how to be a Southern cook."

"Dats right," chimed in Tootsie. "Ja-un don't know nothin' 'bout duh kitchen."

Like every good Southern gal, I obeyed my momma and my other momma, Tootsie—at least when they were watching—but try as I might, I never learned the fine art of Southern cooking. Not to worry, though. My class in cooking Southern cuisine was a'comin.

Some years later, I sat in a circle of chairs with the sweet church ladies of Harmony United Methodist Church at my wedding shower. Between the oohs and aahs, I was handed an oblong box. Suddenly, the room went quiet. All eyes were fixated on me. It was like one of those sacred moments good Christian women live for: altar calls where a family member repents and accepts Jesus as Lord and Savior, Holy Communion when they serve real wine that is not watered down, or that moment after a Church Circle bake sale when the money is counted. Holding that wrapped box, I knew something big was fixin' to happen in my life.

Ripping off the wrapping paper, I found a slab of shellacked, stained wood with lots of drilled holes in it. A separate clear plastic bag contained several wooden pegs. At first glance, I thought it was a larger version of that peg game placed on every table at the Cracker Barrel. You know the one . . . it's there to test your intelligence and patience. So was this gift a version for the less intelligent? Maybe these ladies knew my IQ.

Mama Jewell, my future mother-in-law, noticed the confusion on my face and jumped in to help. "Oh, honey! Mr. Rushton made that for you." Sensing I was still clueless, she continued slowly, "It's a casserole holder, honey, for church covered dishes."

Fear gripped me. My heart raced and beads of mist (never perspiration) formed on my upper lip. Maybe I should have confessed right then that I had never made a casserole in my life and had no intention of doing so. But with the Church Circle ladies on the edge of their seats, eager for my gushing words of gratitude, all I could picture was God saying to me when I reached his pearly gates, "Well done, my domestically challenged servant. In fact, my dear child, most of your efforts were a bit too well done for my taste."

I smiled. I thanked them. They clapped and—thank you, Jesus—we moved on.

With the help of that pegged slab of shellacked wood, I've been saved (cooking-wise) and sanctified. Which is to say I've been transformed into something that can almost pass for a mother and wife who cooks. By the grace of God, I've learned a few tricks for mastering the highly coveted covered-dish endeavors, and believe it or not, I even wrote some recipes that made it into the hallowed pages of our church cookbook, *Cookin' with Harmony*. Maybe it's the names I gave them and not, you know, the actual dishes: Slap Yo' Momma Grits, Resurrection Rolls, Deviled Delilahs (sinfully delicious), and Hoppin' John the Baptist (rice and cowpeas). I'm right proud to be included in such fine company.

So because I'm all about giving back, here are a few covered-dish cooking secrets I've learned. First, show up early. If you want your dish front and center, get there at least fifteen minutes before grace is said. Otherwise, there will be no room left on the main table, and your dish will be relegated to the back table with the store-bought buckets of chicken, rolls, and such.

When I was growing up, there was no such thing as cholesterol. Folks just ate stuff fried in lard and passed out dead from a stroke or heart attack.

We had no idea at the time that their heart trouble was caused by all that fried fatback. But if we had known about cholesterol, my speaker friend Charles Petty claims our mommas probably would have fried it.

After the meat casseroles come the vegetable casseroles, starch casseroles, and finally, the fruit casseroles. Desserts go against the wall on another table. Kids in church learn early to sneak in the side door and fill their pockets with cookies and brownies before slipping out to play tag in the cemetery.

Covered-dish church meals do not have ribbons and awards like you see at a county fair. The grading system is more brutal. To see your dish standing alone minus one glob-full is an announcement to the whole congregation that the dish is not fit for human consumption. Heaven forbid if you use a Pyrex dish with your initials on it.

But I was fortunate. My initials are JH, and so are my mother-in-law's, Jewell Herlong, as are those of my awesome aunt, Josie Herlong. Both these ladies were amazing cooks. So in great big letters, I wrote on the side of my Pyrex dishes, JH. Not saying I was being totally honest. Not saying I wasn't. Just saying . . . sometimes your success comes from how you present.

The best memories of our gatherings are served with some Southern-fried humor. One time, kind and generous Uncle Frank Herlong thanked us for the spaghetti dinner, but in his opinion it tasted "a little sweet." We soon discovered why: Instead of topping his meal with Parmesan cheese, Uncle Frank mistakenly used powdered cream. In another incident, one of our older church members accidentally baked a pot holder into her pineapple casserole. Lots of fiber in that.

With the passing of years, as many of our iconic cooks and characters also passed, I stirred up another scheme to show my respect for their legacy at our gatherings. I stood over my dish and proclaimed, "Wow, this is so delicious. It's almost as good as . . ." and then I'd drop the name of one of our dead cooking legends. Not saying it was honest. Not saying it wasn't. Just saying sometimes the key to success is endorsements.

God bless all of our Southern church sistahs whose covered dishes have a prominent place on the food table, and God help me when my dishes don't make the cut.

Thank the Lord he does not judge us on our ability to win a prominent spot on the covered-dish table of honor. Our ultimate goal should be a seat at the banquet table feasting with our heavenly Father.

12

THE SOUTHERN PREACHER WIFE 2.0

WHEN I WAS A CHILD, our minister's wife wore cotton housedresses, bulky shoes, and a veiled hat to church. She was quiet and sweet; she never rocked the church boat. Boy, how things have changed.

Recently, while speaking at a lady's luncheon, I sat next to a fun, colorful woman. She had blown-out blonde hair, glitter on her eyelids, a big rhinestone ring, and holes in her jeans. As soon as the meeting started, the luncheon organizer introduced the new preacher's wife. The woman next to me stood, turned to the ladies, and waved like a pageant girl. I noticed that she walked funny on her way to the podium.

"Well, I am your new pastor's wife, and if it looks like I'm limping or have blisters, it's because of these new shoes I got from T.J.'s. They're a size too big, so I stuffed toilet paper in them. I know, I know, you're saying to yourself, 'Girl, I don't think I'd have told that.' But I just had to have them. They were 75 percent off." With a big pageant-girl smile she added, "My husband and I are so happy to be serving your church."

Women clapped and laughed. I just had to hear more from this Southern Preacher Wife 2.0 when she sat back down next to me.

"What is the funniest thing you have ever seen?" I asked.

"Well, my husband and I were on the mission field in a revival with some folks from a nearby village. I was all dressed, and my hair was piled in an updo and sprayed with lots of that glue hair spray. As my husband preached, a bird of some kind flew in my hair and got stuck. I jumped up with my hands raised and began screaming. Suddenly, all the other folks in attendance jumped up with their hands raised. Ya know, that is when the revival began. The Spirit moved, sort of like when that dove came down and landed on Jesus. God does move in strange ways and that bird had nowhere to go. It was stuck with me. Sort of like the women in this church are now. And me with these shoes. Now that I've worn them out in public I can't take 'em back. I mean I could, but I wouldn't dare."

I studied the edges of tissue sprouting from the sides of those shoes and thought of how, back in the day, the preacher's wife always carried a pack of tissues in her purse or just one tissue stuffed underneath her watchband for when women in the congregation had a good cry over something gone wrong in their family. Times change, women too.

But one thing hasn't changed. A sweet tea moment with Jesus happens the day we learn to check our pride at the door of the church and be transparent and honest. That'll preach to women every time—and men, if they'll take the time to listen.

Last I heard, my new friend had been stopped for speeding by a police officer. By the time she got through with him, he repented for stopping her, accepted Jesus, and joined their church. Yes, ma'am, we do love our Southern Preacher Wife 2.0.

A Sweet Tea Secret

Many times, people resemble flavors of tea. Some are fruity, others are spicy, and some desperately need sugar. But the best flavor by far is real and all-natural.

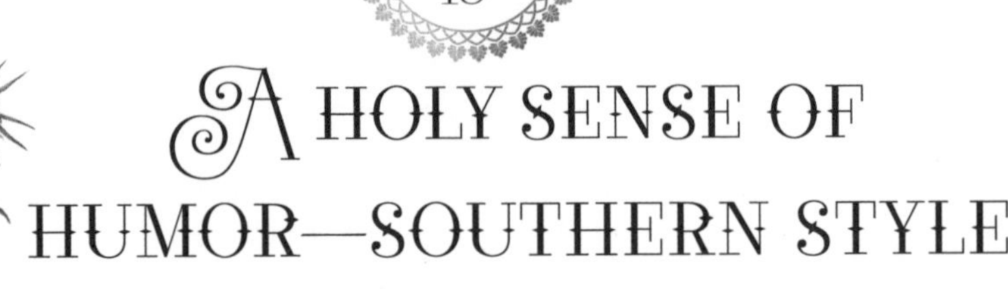

13

A Holy Sense of Humor—Southern Style

As a Southern woman, I can testify that a sense of humor is more valuable than ever. Many times your attitude is more important than designer shoes, clothes, and Botox injections. Can I hear an amen? Or in the style of the Episcopal church, ah-men?

A cousin of mine told me a story about family members years ago who lived in Rockville, South Carolina, and attended Grace Chapel Episcopal Church. Every Sunday, these faithful churchgoers would load up in their mule-drawn wagon and head to church.

One Sunday, as the family made their way to the weekly service, a thunderstorm popped up. The frightened mule made a sharp turn into the entrance to the Presbyterian church, the other church in town. All efforts to redirect the mule failed; from that week on, it refused to ever go any farther down the old dirt road. So for five years, the family attended the Presbyterian church. Finally, one Sunday morning, they made the journey back to Grace Chapel. What changed? They got a new mule.

My very Southern momma always said, "Just find something to make you laugh." With so many challenges in our homes, communities, and workplaces, laughter is super important.

So I wrote *Holy Humor*. Amazing things happen when you develop a sense of humor. One of my passions is speaking and writing about the power of laughter. This passage is my special version of I Corinthians 13. Come on, y'all, it's biblical.

When I speak for lots of folks and do not have a sense of humor, I am just making noise.

If I predict the future and am supersmart and live a faith-filled life but can't laugh, I cheat myself.

If I give food and money to the homeless and talk about being an overcomer of hardships in life but can't laugh, I don't gain a thing.

Humor can deliver you from being jealous. It will shut up boasting and make you think humble thoughts.

If you can laugh your way through life, other folks will want to be your friend. Humor helps you control anger and trash those mental notes of what someone did to you.

Humor laced with truth is powerful. It will protect your mind, give you hope, and help you face adversity with a better attitude.

A good laugh is like a medicine. Proverbs 17:22 says so. Think of being like a child—children love to laugh. So go to the nearest mirror and have a good laugh.

And now these three remain: faith, hope, and love. But one of the greatest gifts you can give to yourself is a sense of humor.

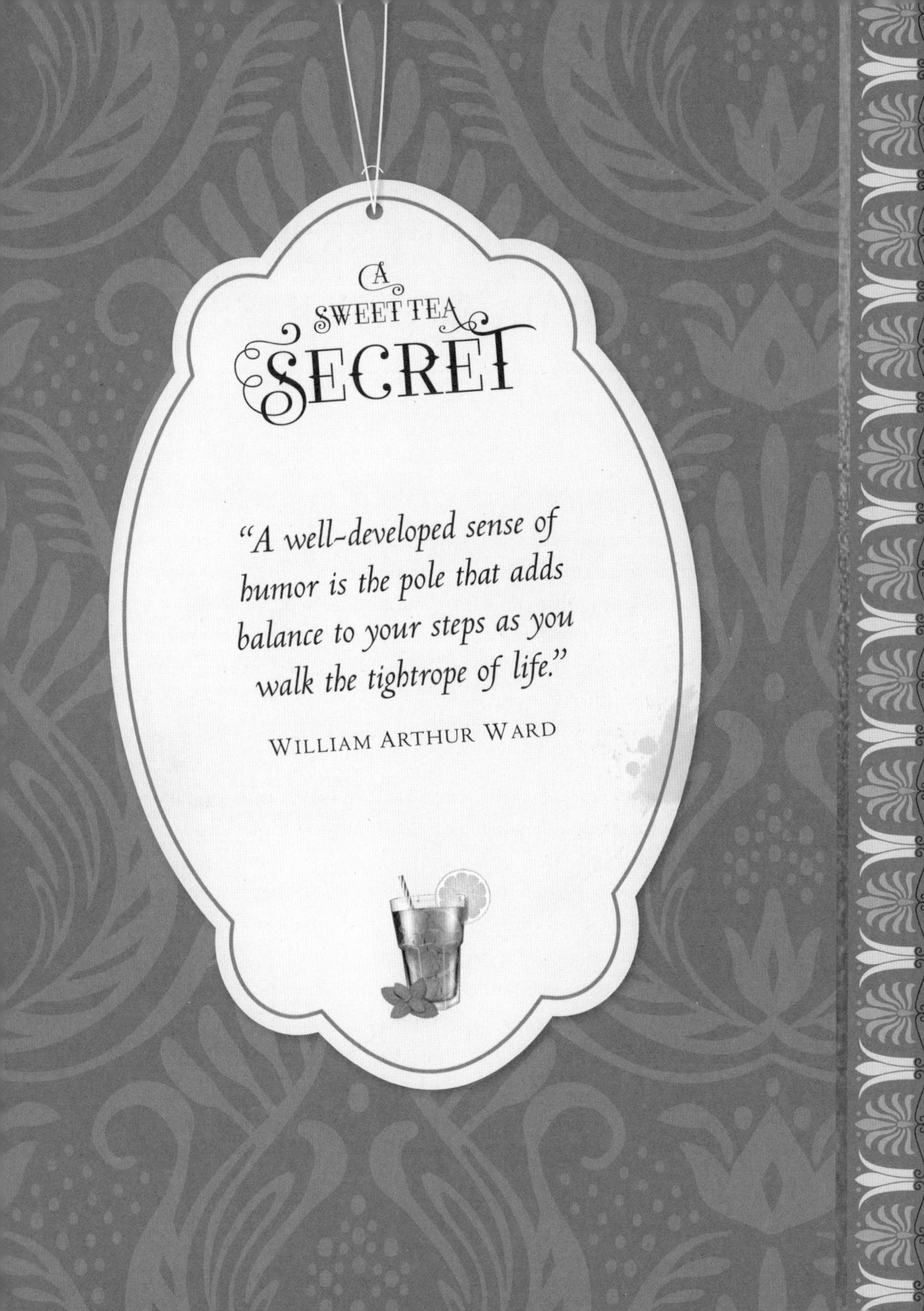
A
SWEET TEA
SECRET
"A well-developed sense of humor is the pole that adds balance to your steps as you walk the tightrope of life."
WILLIAM ARTHUR WARD

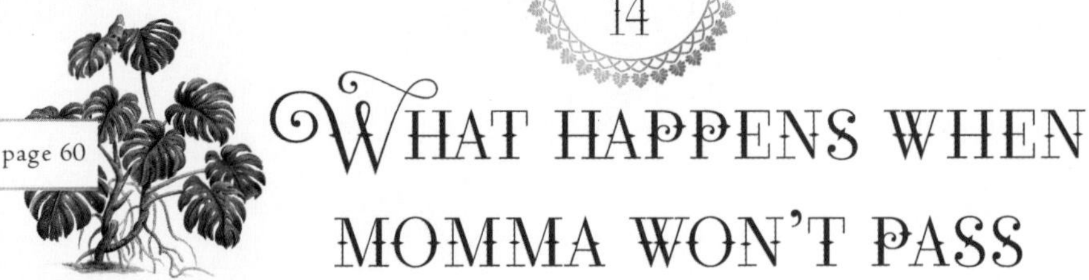

14 What Happens When Momma Won't Pass

Southern folks love to celebrate family, and many have rituals that span decades. My family had a Christmas tradition that lasted close to one hundred years. In the South, death is the only thing that can stop a tradition from happening. For some families, even the passing of a loved one won't stop a beloved family ritual, but it sure can spin into a good tale . . . and an even better sweet tea Southern secret.

This story was told to me by my friend who is a funeral home director.

"Several years ago," my friend said, "a family contacted me concerning a possible passing of their momma. Honey, I ain't makin' none of this up."

Every year, the whole family went cruisin'. They bought their tickets and finalized the details. The one thing they did not plan for was Momma getting sick . . . bad sick.

The children surrounded their momma's hospital bed to say goodbye. Then the cruise topic came up. Right there in front of God and Momma, the family concluded that Momma would want them to go on their trip while the Lord was calling her home.

They called my friend at the funeral home and in the presence of Momma arranged to drop off her burial clothes, jewelry, and teeth. My friend was instructed that when she "passed," to "ice her down" till they got back.

"Well," my friend continued, "them churin' soon discovered that jist 'cause Momma ain't talkin', don't mean she ain't listening."

A funny thing happened during the cruise: Momma did not pass. In fact, she had heard everything they said and knew exactly what was happening.

When the cruise crowd called, my friend shared the news. "Well, your momma was not called home. In fact, she called me. 'I know you got my teeth,' she said. 'I'm hungry, so how 'bout bringing them to me. I am mad, too. I heard everything they said. My churin' asked you to "ice me down" . . . jist like a fish.'"

When the children came to get the rest of their momma's stuff from the funeral home, one of them told me that their momma may have needed them teeth for chewin' food but not for chewin' them out.

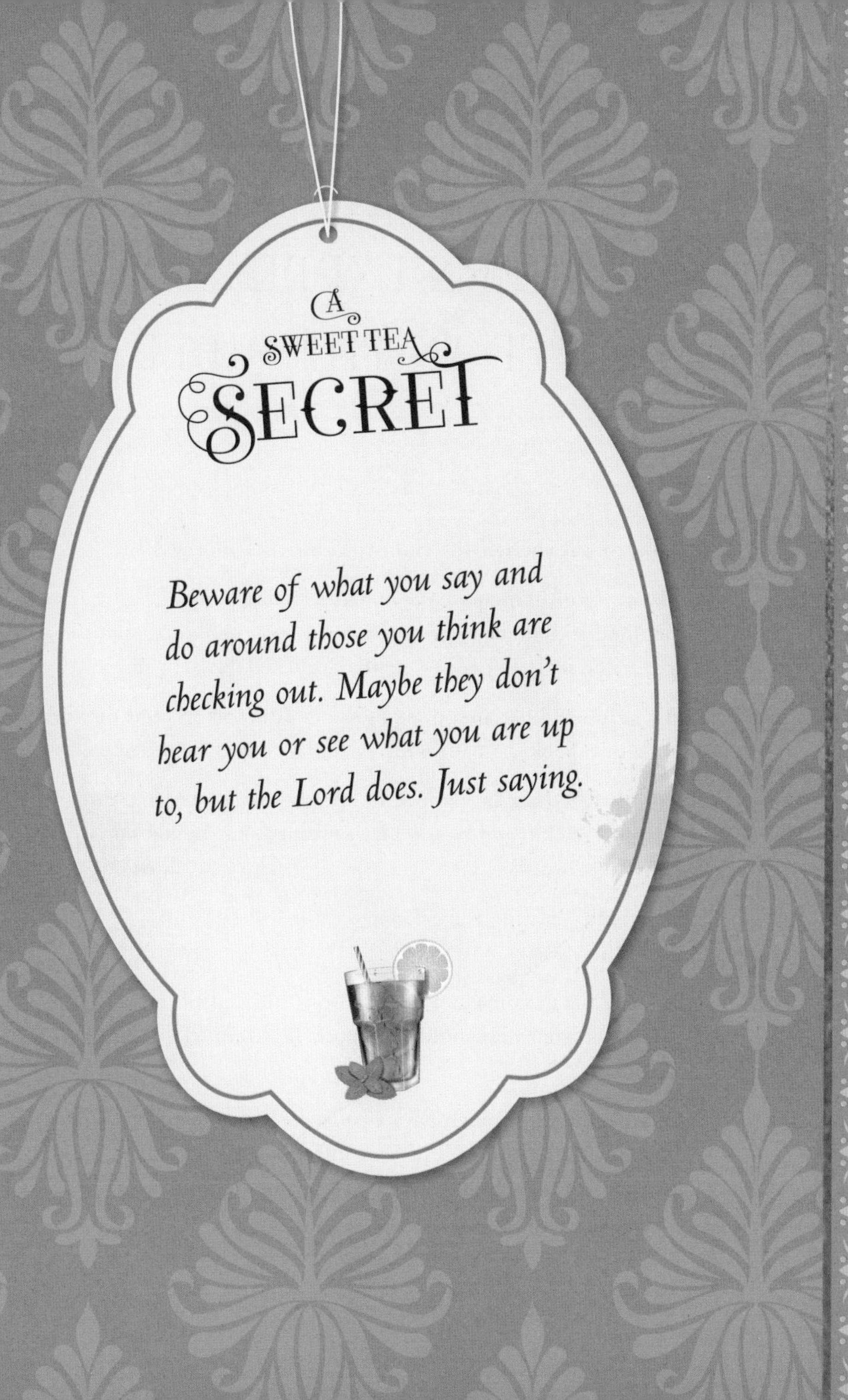
A SWEET TEA SECRET
Beware of what you say and do around those you think are checking out. Maybe they don't hear you or see what you are up to, but the Lord does. Just saying.

15

Southern Expressions Rooted in the Bible

- **Bubba, I tell you what!** ("But mark this." 2 Timothy 3:1)
- **Anyone fixin' barbeque? There better be barbeque.** ("So heap on the wood and kindle the fire. Cook the meat well, mixing in the spices; and let the bones be charred." Ezekiel 24:10)
- **His cornbread jist ain't done in the middle (on account of him come out quick).** ("Eat nothing made with yeast." Exodus 12:20)
- **Lawd have mercy, he escaped by the skin of his teeth.** ("I am nothing but skin and bones; I have escaped only by the skin of my teeth." Job 19:20)
- **Hey, y'all!** ("I bring you good news that will cause great joy." Luke 2:10)
- **How's y'alls momma and dem?** ("Long life to you! Good health to you and your household! And good health to all that is yours!" I Samuel 25:6)
- **Okay, people, we gonna have a come-to-Jesus meeting.** ("Then [Jesus] said to Thomas, 'Put your finger here; see my hands. Reach out your hand and put it into my side. Stop doubting and believe.'" John 20:27)

- **Honey, you're preachin' to the choir.** ("From this time many of his disciples turned back and no longer followed him. 'You do not want to leave too, do you?' Jesus asked the Twelve." John 6:66-67)
- **Grinnin' like a possum eating fire ants.** ("A cheerful heart is good medicine." Proverbs 17:22)
- **He done broke her heart.** ("The LORD is close to the brokenhearted and saves those who are crushed in spirit." Psalm 34:18)
- **I done told you that a snake can't change its spots.** ("Can an Ethiopian change his skin or a leopard its spots?" Jeremiah 13:23)
- **Gnaw on, hit 'em!** ("When they kept on questioning him, he straightened up and said to them, 'Let any one of you who is without sin be the first to throw a stone at her.'" John 8:7)
- **That gal needs to be taken down a peg.** ("If anyone thinks they are something when they are not, they deceive themselves." Galatians 6:3)
- **She'll be nothin' more'n a fly in the soup.** ("As dead flies give perfume a bad smell, so a little folly outweighs wisdom and honor." Ecclesiastes 10:1)
- **Don't you dare go there.** ("But God did say, 'You must not eat fruit from the tree that is in the middle of the garden, and you must not touch it, or you will die.'" Genesis 3:3)
- **Can't you help a brother out?** ("So in everything, do to others what you would have them do to you." Matthew 7:12)
- **She done come off her perch.** ("How the mighty have fallen!" 2 Samuel 1:19)
- **Don't you go puttin' words in my mouth.** ("'Then go to the king and speak these words to him.' And Joab put the words in her mouth." 2 Samuel 14:3)
- **Straight and narrow.** ("Small is the gate and narrow the road that leads to life, and only a few find it." Matthew 7:14)

- **You best wash your hands of the matter.** ("When Pilate saw that he was getting nowhere, but that instead an uproar was starting, he took water and washed his hands in front of the crowd. 'I am innocent of this man's blood,' he said. 'It is your responsibility!'" Matthew 27:24)
- **Wits' end.** ("They reeled and staggered like drunkards; they were at their wits' end." Psalm 107:27)
- **Shoot, the writin's on the wall.** ("Suddenly the fingers of a human hand appeared and wrote on the plaster of the wall, near the lampstand in the royal palace. The king watched the hand as it wrote. His face turned pale and he was so frightened that his legs became weak and his knees were knocking." Daniel 5:5-6)
- **Honey, who are your people?** ("Your people will be my people and your God my God." Ruth 1:16)

My mother had her own sweet tea version of the Bible. She quoted this "verse" that she believed was somewhere in the Bible. "Wives should always take care of their husbands and not neglect romance. For every headache you have, there is a woman out there with an aspirin in her purse."

PART IV

Southern Sistahs

16

Sacred Sistah-Hood

You SPOT THEM anywhere and everywhere. You don't know these women, but as they walk closer, you see their Jack Rogers shoes and their Brahmin, Tory Burch, Michael Kors, or some other designer bag. Pearls gracefully adorn their necks regardless of the outfit, and some even wear fabulous flip-flops. You know designers, and you have learned to spot a real Lilly dress at least 150 feet away. These women's nails are done; highlights and lowlights naturally streak their hair. And thank the Lord, there is no themed clothing . . . blend, blend, blend.

Let me be the first to have the fashion courage to say that if, for example, the season is fall, please do not search for a sweater with fall leaves and wear matching leaves dangling from your ears. Ditch the shoes that look like an array of fall leaves. And do us all a favor—do not wear stretch pants that take front-end loader equipment to hoist them onto your back-end extremities. Jeff Foxworthy said it best on his Blue Collar Comedy Tour: "Bless her heart, them stretch pants did not have a choice." To quote a childhood friend whose mother had a unique way of stating an observation about anatomy: "No one wants to see an outline of your bottom—back or front."

Genuine Southern women learn not to stare; we can sweep another woman without her ever knowing it. The covert once-over is a fine, delicate art handed down by our mothers, grandmothers, and aunts. And believe me, other women are doing the same thing to you. Make eye contact with them, and a bright smile gently spreads across each of your faces. Then another connection—bleached teeth. Who are these women? They are your Sacred Southern Sistahs.

So y'all may be thinking, *Oh, how horrible!* But be honest—we've all been guilty of the "once-over" glance.

If you are fortunate enough to chat with them, you discover they never pay retail. They share their secrets—every detail of how they found their goods and how much they paid to the penny. They are constantly prowling around Pinterest, eBay, and Amazon. They tell you where they found their finery, and they know where you bought your outfit, including shoes and purse. You know they are serious shoppers when they reveal even more secret places: Poshmark, The RealReal, Neiman Marcus Last Call, or T.J. Maxx. They know the day and hour when the delivery truck comes.

But Lord help us if one of our Southern sistahs goes inappropriate on us. If that happens, it's our Southern duty to call her out. White shoes before Easter or after Labor Day are still frowned upon.

Older Southern sistahs may even confess to Botox and Juvéderm treatments. They tell you about the best spray tans or tinted lotion to cover spider veins so you don't have to wear pantyhose during the hellacious summer months. Of course, they also share the latest diets and recipes. They are convinced that the Instant Pot, an AirFryer, and sous-vide cooking are the best inventions since the self-cleaning oven. They know where all the best spas are located too.

If you are fortunate to dive even deeper, Southern sistahs talk about family. These women don't try to impress you with how awesome their families are. Oh no. They will tell you how awful their families are and engage you in a much-needed Southern sistah therapy session.

They tell you about their crazy mother-in-law who was on a Carnival cruise and ran off with one of the hottie tour guides. Then she brought him to the family reunion. The other women in the family acted disgusted but secretly thought they should book a cruise too. And there is that aunt who lives with a guy named Roach. He has one eye and grows questionable herbs in her vegetable garden.

Don't even get her started about her own spawn. You hear phrases like these: "Knock 'em in the head"; "where the sun don't shine"; "never in my life"; "God don't like ugly"; "I love them to death *but*"; and "I tell you what." (What *what* is, no one really knows, but you know to act like you know what *what* is.)

After confessing all the family garbage, a Southern sistah will talk about her latest Bible study. The two of you will quote Scripture back and forth, shed a tear or two, and hug.

The woman you met only minutes ago is now your newest social media friend. You say, "I will pray for you." And when you say it, pray that you won't forget to pray for her. Then both of y'all have to scoot because you are running late . . . again. This is Southern sistah-hood, and she is your newest Southern sistah until the cycle repeats.

Southern sistah-hood is a secret society of Southern women who just get it and get each other.

The good news for women not born in the South is this: There is an adoption process, but we have rules. If you seek admittance—and believe me, you *want* to be in our good graces, else we'll be talking about you; actually, we'll be talking about you anyway, but at least you'll know when and to whom—our secret club is open for membership and we want you to be admitted, not omitted, so here are a few suggestions to consider.

First, we can spot a fake as fast as we can find a no-see-um at dusk.

Second, love and appreciate us, and we will do the same for you.

Third, listen and laugh with us, not at us. We are the only ones who can make fun of our own kind.

Fourth, be yourself and stay yourself. If you're a Yankee, you'll always be a Yankee. But if you're in the sistah-hood, you'll be *our* Yankee, and there's nothing a sistah won't do for another sistah.

Finally, please, for your own good, if you are not from the South, do *not* try to speak Southern. Your tongue is not shaped for it. This, my wannabe-Southern sistah, can lead to "permanent" exclusion. Speak Yankee, but appreciate Southern, and we'll probably love ya till Jesus returns.

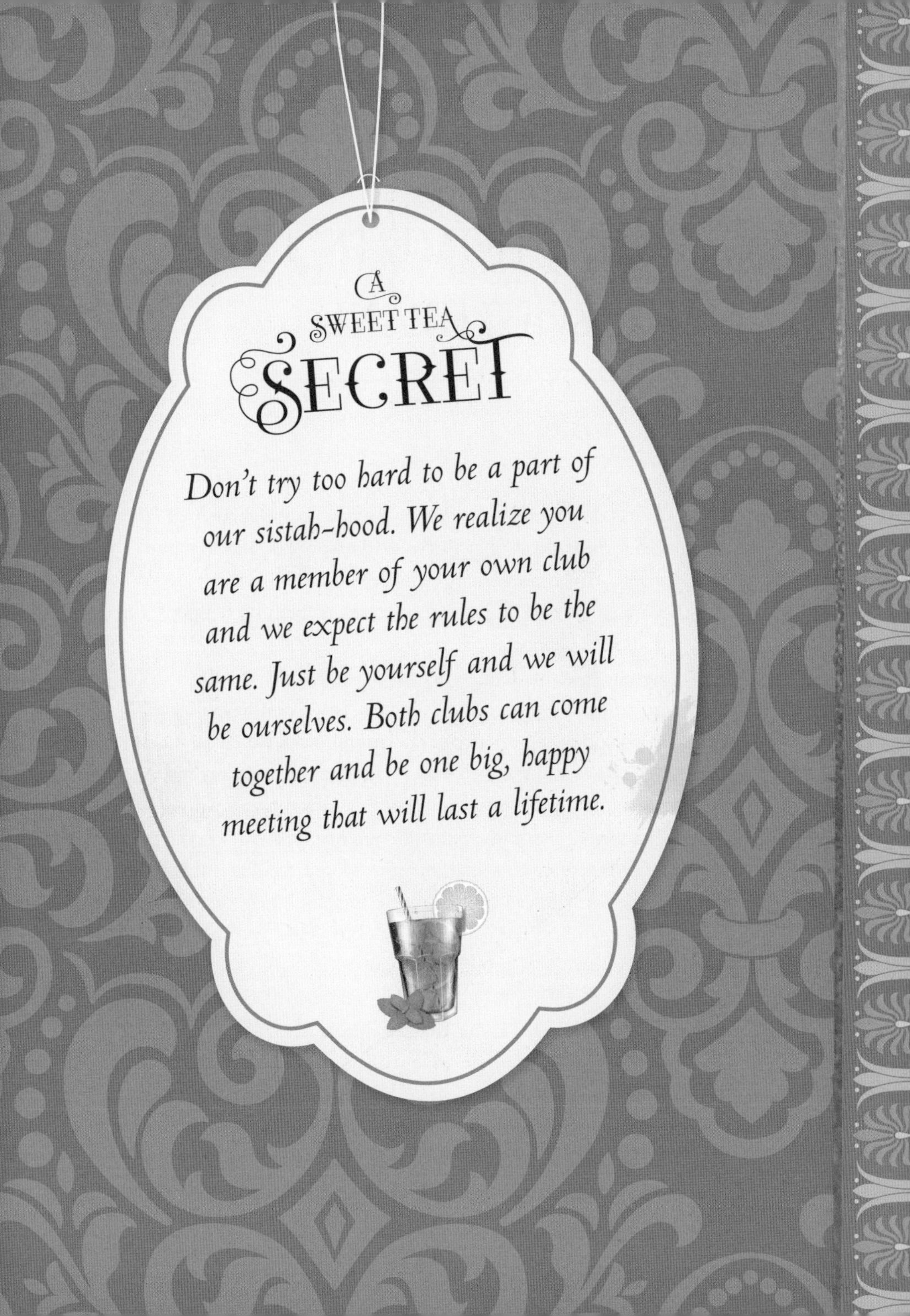

A Sweet Tea Secret

Don't try too hard to be a part of our sistah-hood. We realize you are a member of your own club and we expect the rules to be the same. Just be yourself and we will be ourselves. Both clubs can come together and be one big, happy meeting that will last a lifetime.

17

Sweet Home in the Southland

We all were entertained when we watched *Sweet Home Alabama,* but don't think that Reese Witherspoon's (aka Melanie Smooter's) back-home adventures were too far from the truth. When Southern girls go back home to our roots, something happens. Or maybe I should say nothing happens.

You may have made it to Broadway or starred in a movie, but back home nobody cares . . . except you. You pass the same people growing up and going up as you do coming back down South. In their eyes, you're still the girl who went eggin' with Kenny in his chartreuse Chrysler Charger. You're the same young'un who hid with her BFF under newspapers in Tommy Palmer's parents' wood-grain station wagon, trying to sneak into the Magnolia Drive-in without paying. And remember when you were the talk of the school because you tried to climb to the top of the Coburg Cow on Savannah Highway, only to be stopped by the cops?

But now you have left home and made something of yourself? Yeah, no one has heard about that . . . or cares.

No matter how highfalutin any of us think we are, the back-home folks know we're not all that. So here is a bit of sweet tea wisdom: *No prophet is accepted in his Southern hometown.*

I think what Jesus meant was, you can't escape the bubble you were born in. You can leave, but kinfolk and friends saw you at your best and worst, know your mistakes and lies, and simply accept you as one of theirs. We are too near, too out of focus, so they can't fully grasp our proportions or accomplishments. To those in the bubble, there isn't any considerable difference between you and them.

And really, there isn't. In God's eyes, the one who makes a name for herself in the world and the one who makes a name for herself taking care of her neighbor have equal value. In fact, the one who helps the sick and shut-ins, or the one who bakes cookies for the kids whose mommas can't, may have earned more crowns and bigger crowns than Ms. I'm-So-Full-of-Myself.

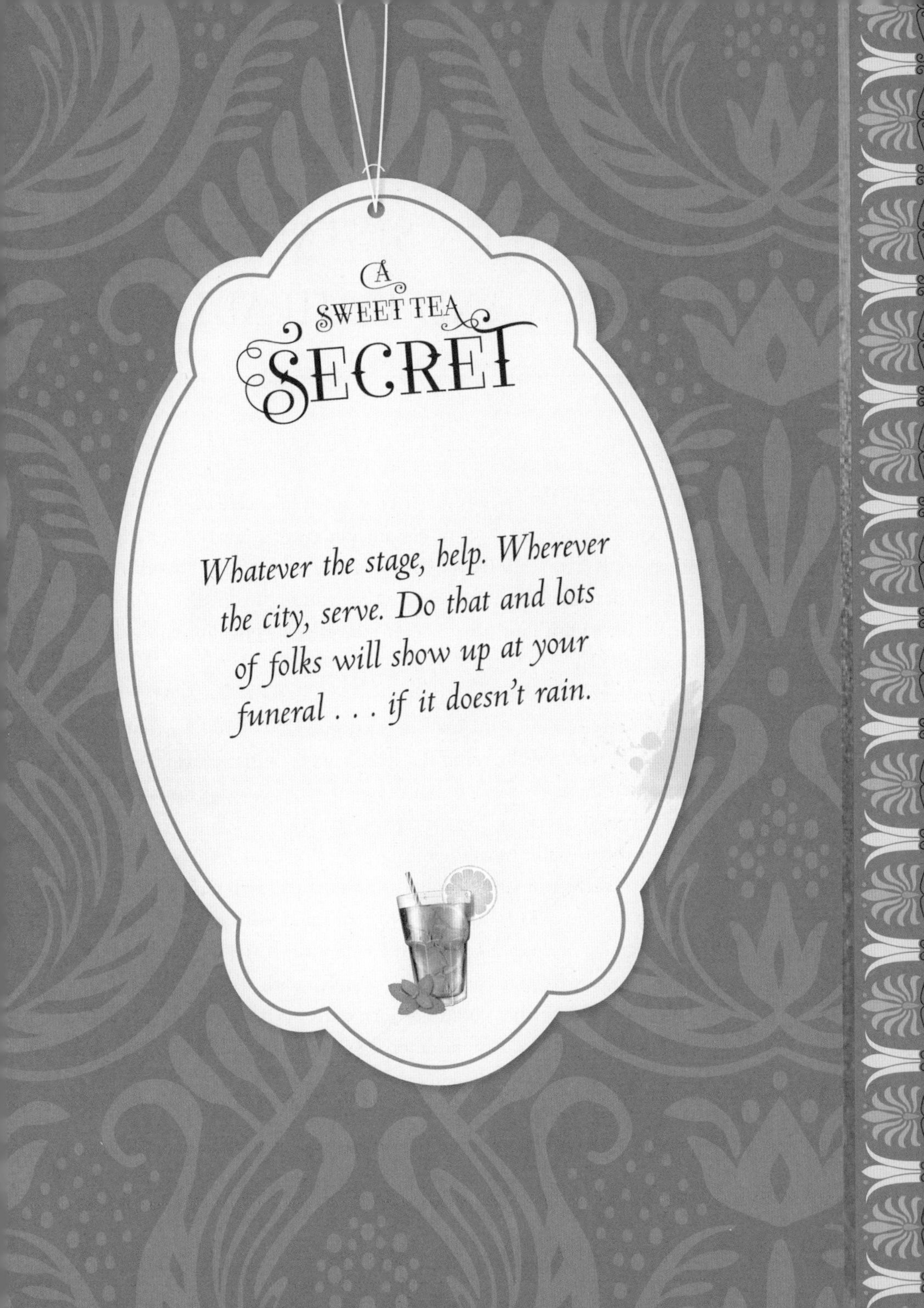

A Sweet Tea Secret

Whatever the stage, help. Wherever the city, serve. Do that and lots of folks will show up at your funeral . . . if it doesn't rain.

18

SOUTHERN SISTAHS IN SICKNESS AND IN HEALTH

IT'S A CODE . . . we Southern women take care of our own. Doesn't matter the place or circumstance, we know how to fix whatever needs fixin'. My friend Charles Petty said it best: "Women live longer than men because of purses." If you need something for a particular ailment, it's in that purse. It may take a while, but you will find it eventually.

On a flight to Dallas, I sat next to an iconic shop owner who clothed the finest women in Augusta, Georgia. One of my sweetest sweet tea moments was learning that trashy women dress for men, classy women dress for women, but those of us who seek ultimate fashion approval dress for "pageant guys."

My seatmate's shop was the mother ship for the fabulous. To be sitting next to this woman was like sitting next to Coco Chanel.

Those of you who follow fashion trends and fashion-world news would recognize her name. Her legendary boutique is located in one of the most exclusive areas of old Augusta. Recently, I'd spied a little black top in her shop that could be worn with practically every outfit. I knew the drill—the end-of-summer 20 percent off sale would become a 50 percent off sale in a few weeks.

Our small Delta plane flew along without trouble for the first part of our flight, and then we hit turbulence. Not from the plane, mind you, but from my unsettled, unfed stomach. I tried not to think

about the rumbling. You know how well that works. To distract myself, I talked with this fashion icon about the elegance of that little black top I'd seen in her shop. But every few seconds my gaze drifted back to the Delta bag in the pocket in front of me.

As if I wasn't feeling bad enough, my mind replayed a horrible incident on another flight a few months earlier. I'd been reading the onboard magazine when some tacky Southern chick, certainly not a Southern sistah, mashed the call button and announced to the entire plane, "This woman is si-uck and throwin' up in this bag. It's gross . . . ya'll hurry . . . I got on a white suit." Of course, her announcement prompted two more passengers to grab their Delta bags.

I'm sure you can guess what happened next on the flight with the fashion icon.

"I'm sorry," I said, cutting her off in mid-sentence, "but I'm going to be sick."

Before I could grab my Delta bag, she handed me hers. "Dah'lin, you do what you have to do."

And I did.

But things only got worse. The woman across the aisle took one look at me and grabbed her *un-swallow* bag. Then the man seated two seats up became sick too. It was a chain reaction like you wouldn't believe or want to see . . . or smell in recycled airplane air.

Suddenly, a cool cloth on my forehead slowed the heated rush that came from the nausea I felt. My seatmate followed this kindness by passing me hand sanitizer and a mint. In her massive purse she'd packed an arsenal of weaponry to fight off any ailment.

She mashed the call button. "I need a co-cola. Not from a can, but a cup half-filled with ice. A real cola, not that diet stuff."

It gets better.

When we landed in Atlanta, she told me to stay seated. Again, the flight attendant was summoned. "I need a car to transport this lady to D-18," the fashion icon said. "There will be no wheelchair assistance, and she is not riding in that annoying beeping car."

Trying to console me after the embarrassing episode, she said, "Honey, that was the most ladylike act of throwing up I have evah seen. And your eye makeup is still fabulous. You come see me next week; that little black top is yours."

Once in the concourse, I was led to the little celebrity car, the one Delta uses to stealthily transport famous people to gates to keep them out of the public eye. The woman driving the celebrity car kept cutting her eyes at me. Finally she said, "I take all the stars to their gates. I just dropped Danny Glover at C-12. I know you from somewhere. Are you a reality TV star?"

I glanced her way and replied, "Only if you count me throwing up on that plane back there as reality-star worthy."

Her mood soured much like my stomach had on the flight. "I hope you don't get sick in my car. I'm picking up Cher after you and don't want her sitting in your throw-up."

While I rode in the Delta celebrity car, I thought about my wonderful friend and how she jumped into action to help me. If ever there was a rock star, she was the real deal. I'm not going to name her shop, but if you're ever in Augusta, Georgia, a local will know.

Many times in the South, some of the best fashion secrets are the sales from fabulous stores, but more valuable than the merchandise is the priceless heart of a genuine Southern sistah in sickness and in health.

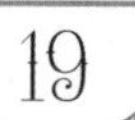

THE SNOOTY PATOOTIE, AKA . . . ANTI-SOUTHERN SISTAH

THERE ARE THOSE we love, honor, and ador-ah in our Southland, and then there are others who test our faith and mess with our heads. However, to these certain folks we owe a debt of gratitude. They helped create our all-time favorite expressions: *Bless their hearts, God love 'em,* etc. Let me introduce you to the Southern snob.

Lest you think I'm judging (which I am), there's a big difference between an elegant, confident Southern sistah and a snooty-patootie pretend wannabe. Daddy used to say, "If a person has to tell you how important they are, they're not."

When I was fourteen, I attended church summer school. A girl sat in front of me who was a card-carrying Southern snooty-patootie. On our first day in class, she swiveled her head in a dramatic fashion and said her last name so loud I thought maybe she was hard of hearing. The snooty-patootie proceeded to tell me that all she wore was Pappagallo shoes, and the only places she bought Pappagallo shoes were at Bob Ellis and Conklin's.

Now, at my innocent, tender age, I had no idea the girl was a snob-snoot, and she was trying to impress me with her South of Broad blue-blood last name and her name-brand designer shoes.

Not really giving a rat's patootie what sort of shoes this girl wore, I asked, "Well, have you tried someplace else?"

"If it's not on King Street, no," Pappagallo princess replied.

Still not connecting the blue-blood dots, I proudly stuck my foot in her face to show her my brand-new pair of penny loafers Momma bought me from Belks in South Windermere.

The look on her face said it all—I was not her kind. She never spoke to me again.

Thank goodness.

And here is the good news: I don't want to be her kind. Her kind is not kind at all.

My closet isn't filled with Pappagallo shoes, but every time I see a pair, I'm reminded to be kind, especially to the folks who are different from me. In other words, don't act like a heel and give them the proverbial boot.

My South of Broad friend Emily lived on Meeting Street, and thank goodness, never once acted uppity. Emily told me that snooty-patootie behavior, if not corrected, can turn a person into a genuine snoot-snob. No kidding.

Several years after my one and only conversation with my summer-school classmate, I had my first encounter with an adult snooty-patootie. Earlier that day, I had been tapped to be in an exclusive pre-debutante club of high school teenage girls, most of whom attended an exclusive private school. It was my first vision of what others thought of me outside of my high school.

After school I visited a boutique loaded with the brand du jour, Villager. The company's signature pin was a small ladybug. I loved Villager clothes and was saving my money to buy a blouse.

I bounced into the shop filled with my exciting news about the club. The clerk, whom I knew, was a middle-aged woman. "Guess what?" I said with great enthusiasm and shared my joy with her.

The woman just stared at me. Her next words still linger in my brain. "You?"

I was so surprised I actually turned around to see who was behind me.

"Well," the older snooty-patootie clerk continued, "aren't you from the islands? I thought this club was exclusive . . ."

Amazing. This older woman was trying to steal the joy of one of my first experiences being recognized as an up-and-coming young woman.

I've learned that these experiences can do one of two things: motivate or paralyze.

And God does show up to prove one of our other favorite Southern phrases: God does not like ugly. The bonus is that he will do our vetting.

So this same snooty-patootie club crowd decided to help themselves to tomatoes in one of my Daddy's fields without his permission. It was after the third harvest, and Daddy had just sprayed the field with an extremely poisonous chemical called Hel-Fire. At the time, that pesticide was the only way to eliminate the large tomato stalks. After ingesting that chemical, it would not take long for those folks to be sniffing roots. Warning signs were posted in the field, but for some reason the posted warnings didn't deter the snoot squad.

A family member of mine saw the snooty vultures in the field with the trunk of a car open, loading up tomatoes, so he decided to teach them a lesson. For the next twenty minutes, he picked tomatoes and helped them load the produce into their car.

As they were getting ready to leave the field, my family member leaned into the car and said, "Promise me you will eat every tomato."

"Oh, we will," chimed in the pack of snobby buzzards.

"Great," he continued. But then he fessed up about the chemical. This family member had previous encounters with other snoots; he knew they probably were immune to poison since they were already infected. As an added bonus, he also told them to trash their clothes and shoes; hmm, I wonder what brand they were wearing?

Eventually I was elected the vice president of that club. Me, the lone Johns Island girl among them.

A sweet tea moment for me is the day I realized that the snooty-patootie attitude has little to do with class and wealth and everything to do with character. *If you think you are somebody, just wait. One day you'll be a has-been, nobody anybody remembers.*

Better to be kind, help others, give generously, and at least try to act humbly than to boast about the shoes you wear or where you live. Your legacy will last much longer than a pair of expensive shoes.

20
Friends and Frenemies

Wise Southern Women learn quickly to keep their friends close, their enemies at a distance, and their frenemies as far as the east is from the west.

Who are your frenemies? A frenemy is a friend-enemy: someone with whom you're friendly, despite a fundamental dislike or rivalry. The absolute worst are the green-eyed frenemies: those who compliment you on your success but secretly hope your next book or speech will flop so they can take your slot. I study successful women, and the reality is this: If you step out and step up, you will become a target of your frenemies.

Other women come up to me all the time complimenting me on what I do, what I've achieved. "Blah, blah, blah . . . Jane, you are a singer, writer, author. You are *soooo* funny," et cetera. When a frenemy says something like that, she's thinking, *I soooo want to strangle you right now.*

Come on, you know what I'm talking about. You've thought it about someone you call a friend. I know I have.

But the truth is, we're all failures. And successes. Unfortunately, our failures seem to define us more than our successes. At least in our own minds.

Here's a list of my epic flops:

- I was placed in the slow section in first grade. It was first grade, for crying out loud! How could I be behind and slow before I even

began? I blamed it on my big lips and tomboy attitude. Of course, that only opened me up to more teasing. My parents feared I would follow in my siblings' footsteps since they struggled in school too. I'm from South Carolina and folks in the South do everything at a slower pace, so maybe my teachers were right. Plus, there might have been some cousin inbreeding happening on the branches of my family tree that originally was more like a wreath. And there was no bridge to the mainland.

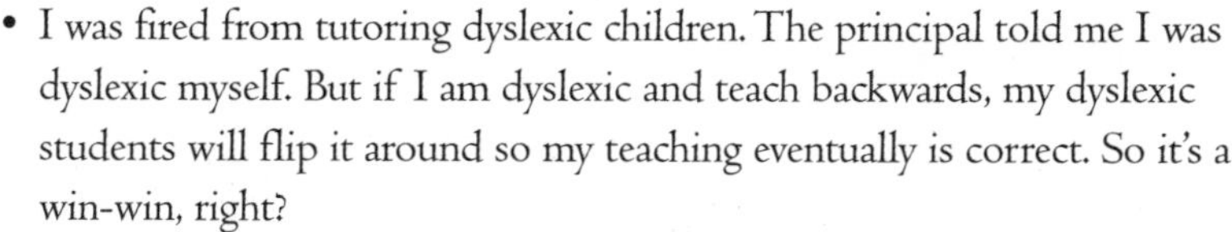

- I was fired from tutoring dyslexic children. The principal told me I was dyslexic myself. But if I am dyslexic and teach backwards, my dyslexic students will flip it around so my teaching eventually is correct. So it's a win-win, right?
- Given that I started out at the bottom of my first-grade class, had big lips and fists hard enough to wallop boys, and a low IQ (whatever that means), of course I ended up with low SAT scores in high school. Here's the thing: I SAT a lot in high school . . . summer, winter, spring, and fall. You'd think that someone who SAT as much as I did would have a higher SAT score, but it turns out sitting wasn't enough. You actually had to learn . . . stuff. (I was going to use another word, but my deceased mother would have come out of her grave and suggested a stronger word.)
- I had low IQ and low SAT scores, so my next challenge was college admission. One poor institution that desperately needed my parents' money agreed to take me under "academic probation." I felt like I'd done something wrong before I even started. Made me feel like I was back in first grade all over again. My writing professor gave me an F in writing. But years later, I presented him with a copy of my first book, *Bare Feet to High Heels,* in front of the entire Columbia College student body. *Sweet.*
- I was rejected by an agent who didn't think my comedy was right for SiriusXM radio. Guess he didn't think I was *Sirius* enough.

Now, here's the list of what those "failures" did for me.

- I became Miss South Carolina and a contestant in the Miss America Pageant.

- In the pageant, I was the fake Miss Congeniality, which means I walked the iconic convention center's 400-foot ramp with the Miss America crown on my head for TV rehearsals (the Miss America production company's equivalent for Miss Congeniality).
- I made the dean's list before I graduated from college.
- My peers awarded me top honors—May Queen and Most Womanly. (I'm glad they did not check my ability to have young'uns, since birthin' was a seven-year journey for me.)
- I became the bestselling author of four books and received a major publishing contract from Hachette, one of those big publishing houses out of New York City.
- I was accepted into graduate school.
- I was inducted into the Speaker Hall of Fame.
- I performed twice at Radio City Music Hall.
- My comedy is played on SiriusXM Radio.

My point is this: Most folks don't know diddly-squat about you. And those who know diddly-squat about you are sometimes green with envy because you've turned your mess into a message. With every epic failure that could have beaten me down, I said to myself, "I will prove them wrong; they have no idea the fight I have inside of me." I love this quote: "It's not the size of the dog in the fight, it's the size of the fight in the dog."

When you become the talk of whatever, remember the frenemies are out there waiting for you to flop, so smile and walk on or flip it around. That's what Jesus did, and it worked for him.

Well, until they killed him.

Which only proves my point: Frenemies will crucify you if you're not careful.

Some parting wisdom from my daddy, Benjamin Roper Jenkins, and from Tootsie: "You pass the same people going up as you do coming back down" and "Sum time yo spirit and dey spirit don' like one 'nother."

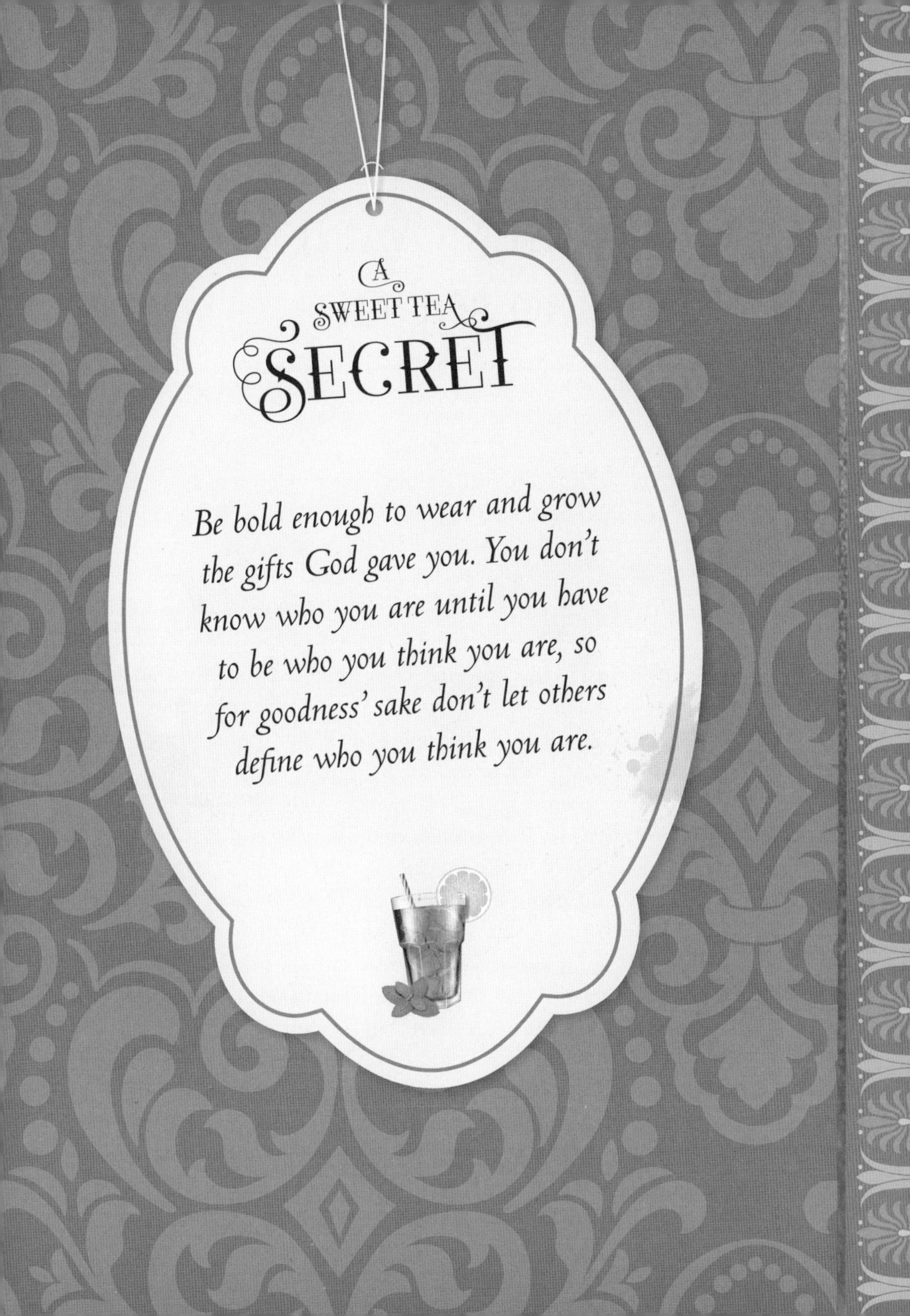
A
SWEET TEA
SECRET
Be bold enough to wear and grow the gifts God gave you. You don't know who you are until you have to be who you think you are, so for goodness' sake don't let others define who you think you are.

21

When Ovaries Go South

SOME OF YOU will get this right away because you totally understand. Yet some Southern sistahs need a little more 'splaining, so here ya go.

I have a theory: As our bodies age and change *again,* strange things happen . . . again. I remember a horrible woman who mouthed off to a sweet clerk twenty years ago. I did the Christian thing and even apologized to that dear store clerk while declaring that I would never act like that awful, tacky woman. But somehow, for some reason, I find myself slowly becoming her. Words fly out of my mouth I can't stuff back or unhear.

Some of you may rewind that fabulous parking space scene from the movie *Fried Green Tomatoes* and secretly desire to change your name to Towanda.

There just comes a time in life when Southern belles become like the Liberty Bell . . . we crack. But hallelujah! We are free at last and liberated! Plus, my momma did not rear a wimpy woman.

I struggled with this concept since Thomas, my moral compass, suggested I delete this newly discovered *aha* moment. He scolds me when I mouth off or try to act like a steel magnolia with an attitude. But late one night either God, my mother, or my grandmother (maybe all three) woke me up from the dead of sleep. And I remembered who first taught me about what can happen when ovaries go south.

My sister and I were young when my grandfather passed away suddenly. Being sweet girls, we spent the night with my grandmother to comfort her in her frail state.

Picture this: Grandmother McElveen was the poster grandma for the universe—cotton housedress, pre-SAS shoes (more hideous than SAS), and soft gray hair that on occasion turned a shade of Senior Citizen Blue. (I'm convinced that's a real shade of Lady Clairol.)

After a delicious meal that only a seasoned grandmother can cook, we all settled down for the night. But outside, trouble was brewing. Around midnight, we were awakened when a stranger beat on the locked screen door yelling, "Let me in! Let me in!"

My sister and I grabbed each other and screamed. We knew our job was to protect our sweet, elderly grandmother.

"You get away from here!" said a strange voice with a low growl.

Grandmother McElveen must have called a man to protect us, I thought.

The beating on the door continued and so did more threats from our protector. My sister and I mustered the courage to peek around the bedroom door to see this "man" in action. What a shock! There stood our sweet grandmother wearing her robe and signature hairnet.

Like a scene straight out of *Bonanza,* Grandmother McElveen planted her legs ready to fight and pulled a Browning Lever-Action Rifle tight into her shoulder. "Get off my porch or I will blow your head off!"

My sister and I were more stunned than the intruder. He took off in a full sprint from the house, and we ran full throttle back into the bedroom and hid under the sheets.

Stocking feet padded on the floorboards and then that sweet grandmother voice: "Dah-lins, are y'all okay?"

That night our sweet, frail grandmother taught us that sometimes the most effective results are bullets that come from a commanding voice and a lever-action rifle.

After my grandmother etched that memory into my brain, I knew my mother would be the next memory-maker reminder.

Back in college, I picked enough tomatoes one summer to feed a small country. Daddy was delighted since my hard work covered living expenses

for a full year at college. When registration for the summer classes began, I needed a music/arts class, and Daddy, to my surprise, agreed to let me study in Europe for the summer. My only hesitation was the fear that one of the elderly members in the family would pass away while I was on the trip. Momma promised that if anything terrible happened, she would let me know.

London was the last stop on our trip. In a week, my parents would meet me at the Charleston airport. I phoned home one last time to remind them of my arrival details. The conversation went something like this:

"Hey, Momma! Everything good at home?"

"Yes, things are okay."

Hmmm. *Okay* was one of Momma's code words. "Okay? Is anyone dead?" (Time is money when calling internationally, so get to the point.)

"We'll see you in a few days. I got arrested yesterday. Bye."

"What?"

In a nutshell, Momma and Grandmother McElveen were on the way to the doctor when Momma (Eleanor) ran a yellow light. Police sirens wailed, Eleanor was pulled over, and the words flew. She mouthed off to the policeman. Daddy always said that a bottle of Tabasco would not affect her tongue since it was already on fire. Basically, that cop got a tongue-lashing, and that hot tongue got Eleanor parked in the back seat of a police car. All I can say is, God help the man, policeman, person, or whomever who messes with Momma and Grandmother McElveen.

The rest of the story? Eleanor was released without bail. But her tongue and fighting spirit were never tamed. This tenacity served my mother well, especially after my father passed away. Daddy was a giver to his own demise, and Momma disagreed with some of his decisions. Riding to Daddy's funeral, Momma clarified her new rules: "Children, there is a new sheriff in town. The Bank is closed. Get used to it." In Momma's defense, she was generous in many ways.

Ready for a super sip of strong tea?

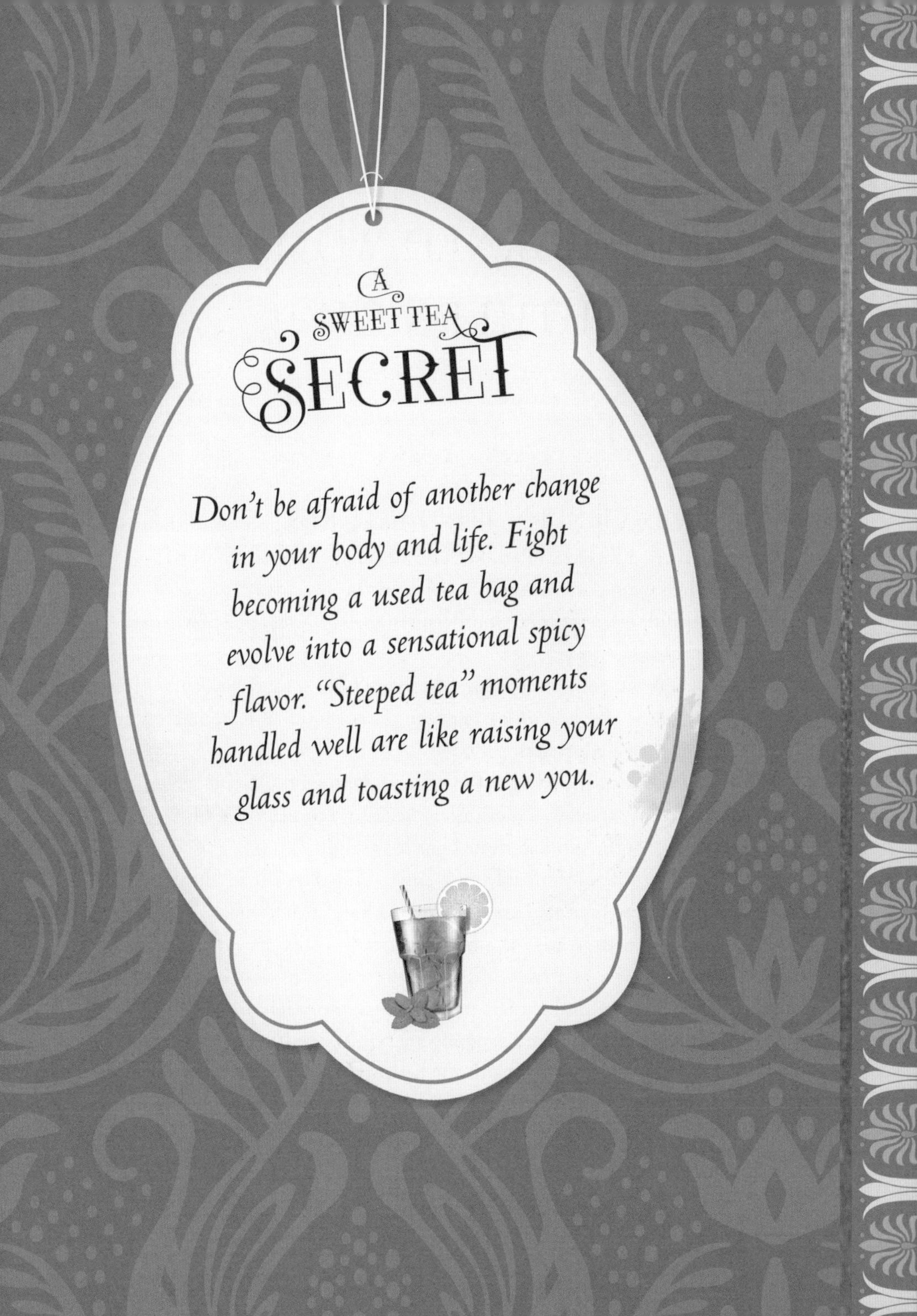
A
SWEET TEA
SECRET
Don't be afraid of another change in your body and life. Fight becoming a used tea bag and evolve into a sensational spicy flavor. "Steeped tea" moments handled well are like raising your glass and toasting a new you.

22
The Scorned Woman—Southern Style

You've seen the pictures and heard the stories of scorned women. "Hell hath no fury like a woman scorned"—so the saying goes. Chilling words, but the sweet tea secret of a beautiful, once-scorned Southern sistah is . . . well, maybe it's best if you read her story.

Dale was only seventeen, but she felt like a modern-day Cinderella. The captain of her high school football team had invited her to their high school prom.

Oh, what a magical night this will be, she thought. Of course, her dress was perfect, shoes awesome, every accessory in place. Her hair, skin, eyelashes—the girl had done herself up right.

Then the unthinkable happened. Only days before the prom, her prince backed out. "Sorry," he said, "I have another date." What he didn't say with words but said in silence was this: *You aren't pretty enough for me.*

Her heart broke. Her spirit died—or so it felt.

Years later I was visiting my friend Dale in Nashville. We were shopping for the perfect suit for her to wear at the cover photo session for her book. As soon as Dale stepped out of the dressing room, wearing that pea-green molded silk suit, my jaw dropped. She was stunning.

Over the years, Dale had evolved into a drop-dead gorgeous professional speaker and author who spins a tale so well that event planners clamber to book her. With her good looks and way with words, Dale enjoys all the trappings of a beautifully balanced, successful businesswoman.

The next time we were together, some months later, I learned more of the story. "Jane," Dale said to me, "I may look like I have it together now, but I didn't start out this way. Let me tell you how all this started."

And she did, recounting her high school prom disaster.

"But then," she said, "you know how we Southern sistahs turn rejection into injections of fire and fury. Remember the suit we bought together? During my book signing tour, I wore it at the stop at the Tupelo, Mississippi, library. I was sitting behind a table signing my new book when I heard *him,* only mostly what I heard was 'ahem.' Girl, when I looked up, there he stood, the fool who broke my heart. And oh honey, let me tell you, he was a looker. A pig-cooker looker. I'm not going to call him fat, because I'm not into fat-shaming, but God love him, his gene pool needed a lifeguard. Middle-aged, but then so am I, but I still got all my hair. He left his in that too-big-for-his-head football helmet he wore, I guess, 'cause he was bald as a cue ball. And successful? The boy was living with his mommy and daddy. So there he was staring at me with his mouth open and wearing that old letter jacket that was at least three times too small."

"You enjoy telling this story, don't you?" I said.

"Every time, sister. Every time. Let me tell you, it was a magical moment. Twenty-plus years late, but magical just the same."

"Did the two of you go off and catch up?" I said, sarcastically egging her on to spill it all.

"Catch up, my foot. I took a look at Mr. Football Star of yesteryear, and after a long, glorious pause, I gracefully pushed back my chair, stood, and walked around to the front of the table. I straightened the wrinkles from my outfit so every part of me was curved to perfection. Then I studied his eyes while he got an eyeful of my pea-green molded silk suit. Finally, he said those words I longed to hear long ago, 'Uh, I ah . . . made a mistake.'

"I think my posture and body language said it all . . . without words."

Sometimes all we need is a little rejection to force us to rechannel our wrath into positive improvements. After getting dumped, Dale didn't become bitter. She became better—a better person, a better writer, a better speaker, a better friend.

Hell hath no fury like a woman scorned. But heaven hath no joy like a woman vindicated.

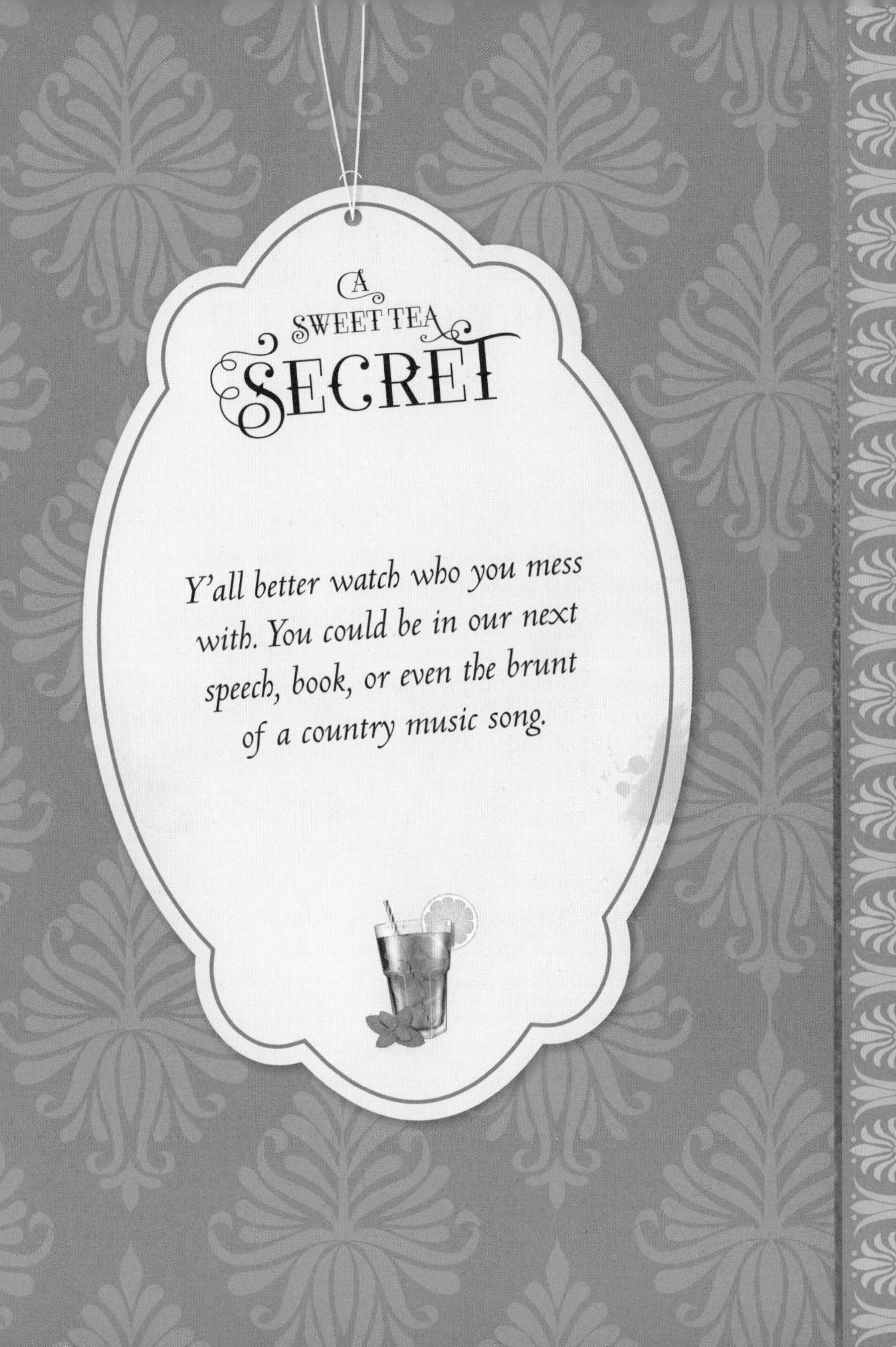
A
SWEET TEA
SECRET
Y'all better watch who you mess with. You could be in our next speech, book, or even the brunt of a country music song.

23 When the Southern Sistah Womans Up

A FEW SUMMERS AGO, I had a bit of a female-parts scare. My gynecologist discovered a growth in my right ovary. "We don't know what it is, but it's growing," he said.

Right out of my unfiltered mouth, I heard myself say, "Oh, I know what it is. I've grown a testicle."

I actually thought my gyno-guy was going to recommend that I visit the tenth floor for a psychiatric evaluation. What I did not tell my gynecologist is that I had to learn to set boundaries and to grow up when I wanted to throw up. That sweet, compliant beauty queen in me had to learn life skills to survive many tough years.

Lose a job? Passed over for a promotion? No help at home cleaning, cooking, bathing the kids, mowing the yard, fixing the garbage disposal, balancing the finances, getting the oil changed in your vehicle? Stop whining and start winning.

If you keep calling your girlfriend over and over to recount the same, sad woe-is-me story, it's past time to tell your sorry self to hush! If no one calls you when you're in a tough spot, odds are they're sick of the whining. Haven't heard from your friends in a while? They're having lunch and shopping without Debbie Downer because you ruined the last fun girlfriend trip. Learn to handle your emotions, or your emotions will handle you.

Look, I get that we sistahs are comrades in arms; and by arms

I mean we hug each other and cry on each other's shoulders. But there comes a time when we need to wipe off the smeared mascara, put away the tissues, and woman up.

Let me be so bold as to say that some of today's touted feminists have it all wrong. Women do not need to be like men. We do not need to take the power of men or ridicule men or crush men under our high heels. The glass ceiling is not something to be broken; it is the crystal flooring beneath our feet when we reach female excellence. You are destined to become a warrior princess and not a wimpy worrier. You know this deep in your soul. Or did as a little girl. Begin to live like it.

We women have all the power we need and more. When God made us in his image, he gave us his power, his beauty, his empathy for others, his compassion and caring. He made men in his image, too, but that was his first attempt. After God took one of Adam's ribs, his second attempt was new and improved.

Naomi, Ruth's mother-in-law? I view her as middle-aged and maybe even going through THE CHANGE. She had a change, all right; she lost her husband and sons and found herself with no means of support in the midst of a famine. Naomi even changed her name to *Mara,* which means "bitter" (Ruth 1:20-21, AMP). Thank goodness, her pity party did not consume the rest of her life; she parted ways with her problems and set out to find solutions. Naomi changed her perspective and became a bold woman.

Esther, queen of the Persian Empire? She became a hero when she saved her uncle Mordecai and her people, the Jews, from genocide. Esther was beautiful and courageous.

Hannah, the mother of Samuel? She inspired me because I also had trouble conceiving a child. Hannah gave birth to a son who became one of God's greatest prophets. Even though the other women in the village taunted her for being childless and despite her husband's complaint that he was worth more to her than ten sons, still she prayed to God day after day for a child. And God heard her prayer. Hannah was persistent and prayerful.

Let me be totally blunt: Thank God for personal battles that can become teachable moments. You will discover who you are and hopefully

learn how to handle the next issue. Earn your way to a PhD of emotional balance. If not, expect PhD to take on another meaning . . . pills, heartaches, and depression.

So there, I said it—something I've been wanting to say for a long time.

How about you? Stop trying to be a man and become the woman God intended you to become. Do that and you'll find you have more power and prestige than you'll ever need. Looking for inspiration? Check out the accomplishments of our biblical *she-ro* sistahs or WWWs—Wonder Women of Wisdom.

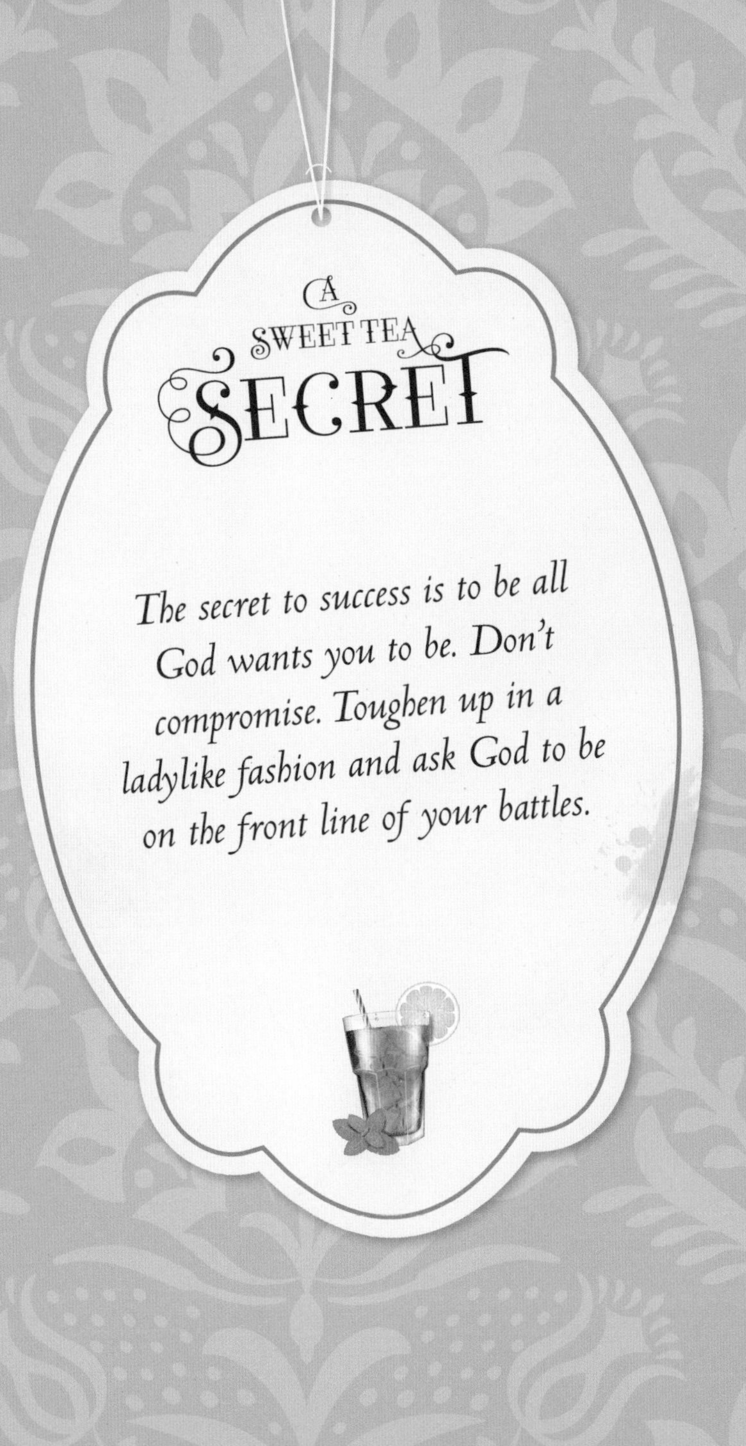

A Sweet Tea Secret

The secret to success is to be all God wants you to be. Don't compromise. Toughen up in a ladylike fashion and ask God to be on the front line of your battles.

PART V

SOUTHERN SHOW-OFFS AND SHOWDOWNS

24

OW-AH SOUTHERN HOMES AND GARDEN SHOW-OFFS

THOMAS AND I had been engaged for one week when the talk of our home came up. The topic was quite the talk of the town since we had also only known each other for a week. The story of our romance is in *Rhinestones on My Flip-Flops*. You'll definitely want to buy a copy in order to read the salacious, not to mention scandalous, details. (Not really—our dating was pretty tame compared to what young'uns do these days.) I will say that when you pray for Jesus to quicken your heart and Mr. Right says, "Hello," not only is your heart quickened but also your engagement, wedding, and a lot of other events you didn't anticipate.

My phone rang. "Jane, this is your fiancé." Since we were still getting acquainted, apparently Thomas felt it necessary to introduce himself. "Do you want to build a house or renovate an old Southern home?"

This was another of those Jesus moments: The desire of my heart had always been to live in an old Southern home.

"Renovate, of course!" I was so totally naive.

"Well, I talked to Mr. Jeff, who owns that historic house down by the soybean field on the farm. He said we can buy the place for five hundred dollars."

"Five hundred or five hundred thousand?"

"Hundred."

"What's the catch?" I was thinking Thomas was my catch, which meant a home for five hundred dollars was too much of a blessing to expect from God.

"We have to move it off of his land."

For a moment, I visualized a double-wide Southern home . . . on wheels.

How much trouble can that be? I thought. *Or cost?*

Of course, we bought the house. Did I mention I was totally naive? The back of the house was built before the Revolutionary War, and the main part of the house was attached with a breezeway in 1870. Then a porch was added in the 1900s. The entire house was moved in two pieces and became the Harmony Community's event of the season—some of Thomas's family had a picnic on the farm as they watched the house being moved across the fields.

After we knocked down the chimneys, replaced the plaster with Sheetrock, and added the bathrooms, it was all ours—a complete and total mess to renovate. Did I mention that we had no money? We had no money! Thomas spent two months staining the kitchen cabinets, and I painted the entire inside of the house Navajo White. If the phrase Navajo White offends anyone, I apologize. That was the color on the can. I did not name the can or color. I simply painted. And painted. And painted until I was Navajo White.

One day Thomas stopped by to see how I was doing with painting—the entire house. Frustrated and exhausted, I sat on the floor and cried. "Thomas, I need help," I said, wiping sweat from my upper lip. "These ceilings are high, and I can't reach the top of the walls."

"Oh, honey, don't cry. I'll get you some help."

Thomas—that charming Southern man sent by Jesus to rescue my heart from a life of loneliness, my hero and soul mate and the frugal one in our relationship—bought me a roller extender.

We worked from the back of the house to the front and finished the rooms upstairs. Many years passed before we could afford the help of a professional decorator.

When it comes to hiring a decorator, I cannot erase the memory of my mother hiring a professional, renowned Charleston designer many years ago.

Some Southern men love to show their kill by hanging animal heads all over the family room. But not my Daddy. He decorated with fish: a mako shark over the mantel, a wahoo over the window by the television, a red snapper in the kitchen, and the mother fish of them all, a sailfish, from a trip to Acapulco hanging over the couch.

Momma made sure Tootsie fried her signature spiced chicken, which filled the house with aromas that put diffused essential oils to shame. Add a rice steamer filled with Charleston red rice, a cooking tin filled with biscuits, and some vegetables in the pressure cooker, and life is good. The day had to be perfect.

Momma, Tootsie, and I were on high alert when the front doorbell rang (two dings instead of one) and the blue-blooded, iconic interior designer entered our house. To add to the drama, the woman wore a colorful scarf that had to have been purchased on King Street at Elza's, and her shoes were definitely from Bob Ellis.

She went through our modest brick ranch-style home as if it were a historic mansion on the SOB (South of Broad) section of the Charleston peninsula. All was well until Daddy walked into the house for "dinner." The decorator could not have said anything worse: "Well, those fish have got to go."

My quiet, sweet father reared his head from his red rice and fried chicken and said, "No, the first thing to go will be you."

Then Tootsie piped in and pretty much said it all. "Do Jedus. Dem fish gwine stay right on duh wall." And she was right. To this day, the mako shark and the sailfish are hanging in the family room, and Gawd help us if they are moved.

Southern women understand that your home may be filled with the finest designer décor, but if you desire a sweet home, there must be a place for roadkill or other prize catches on the wall.

A SWEET TEA SECRET
Choose well; better to display a trophy fish than be replaced with a trophy wife.

25

From Beatrix Potter to Something Hotter

THOMAS AND I INVITED a Southern interior designer into our home—she was stylish, charmin', and totally delightful. The best part was the way she "worked" Thomas. Girls, if you can find a Southern interior designer who can "work" your husband, you can have the home of your dreams. You may not be able to afford it, but with the right words from the right Southern designer, you'll have it.

The amazing part about my Southern interior designer was that even while wearing her working clothes and getting dirty, her hair and makeup were impeccable. She never perspired. In the South we vow and declare that we never sweat; we mist and then glow.

I had no idea how she would convince Thomas to spend the money required to do the things she insisted needed to be done, especially when Thomas could do them himself. I know very little about how men think. But I've noticed that when a man thinks he can do something, he'll refuse to pay someone else to do it. Like, say, the oil needs changing in your car. You could pay one of those quick-oil-change shops to drain and replace the oil and filter and be out of there in thirty minutes (or less). But if your husband hears you're even thinking about foolishly spending that kind of money (an amount that is like a tenth of what we women spend on a trip to a nail-and-hair salon), he'll promise to "get to it" when he has the time.

As our Southern interior designer walked through our home, no words were exchanged—just low-volume sounds. Her gestures were dainty, complemented with sighs and slight head-nodding: signs of her approval. No one knew what she was thinking until suddenly, in a dramatic fashion, her head swiveled. She stood in her signature pose with the confidence of a contestant making her final walk down the runway at the Miss America Pageant. Her next words inspired a moment of decision for Thomas.

"Well . . ." she drawled as she placed her perfectly manicured hand on my treasured antique credenza (given to us by a family who wanted to get rid of it), "I declare, Thomas. I do believe we have fi-nan-cially outgrown this piece of furn-i-chure." What happened next can only be described as a miracle.

"Okay. Just do what you have to do," said Thomas.

And so the gutting began.

Years passed. After the entrance hall and upstairs were completed, the next room on the list was our daughter Caroline's bedroom. Here is where the Southern momma struggles. We can hardly tolerate our baby girls growing up, and we hold on to every stitch of their childhood. I mean everything.

Caroline's nursery was precious. Beatrix Potter characters filled the room along with a Ms. Noah's Southern Belle Bunny doll, wearing a strand of pearls, of course. But the finishing touch was the Beatrix Potter border print around the ceiling. Oh, how adorable. And the memories. Tossing Ms. Noah's Southern Belle Bunny was almost as heartbreaking as watching my precious Caroline leave for preschool. Granted, Caroline was in junior high at the time of the interior decorator's visit and blossoming into a young woman, but my precious, always compliant Southern-belle-in-training had never complained about her Beatrix Potter border print.

Enter our interior designer. "Caroline, honey," dripped her drawl, "would you like to have a big-girl room befo-ah you go to college or get married?"

Our pale-yellow nursery with the Beatrix Potter border print became a pea-green room with deep-brown burlap window cornices slightly trimmed

with jungle print, and in mandatory Southern style, monogrammed with "ECH" in hot pink. A beautiful, petite crystal chandelier hung in the corner. To complete the festive look, I found a large chair in the shape of a giant high heel at Big Lots that was covered in—you guessed it—jungle print.

Not saying buying the giant high-heel chair was one of my proudest moments, but it made the room. And when you're a Southern Homes and Garden Show-Off host and homeowner, no expense is too little, too much, or too bold.

Southerners love to decorate, regardless of the season.

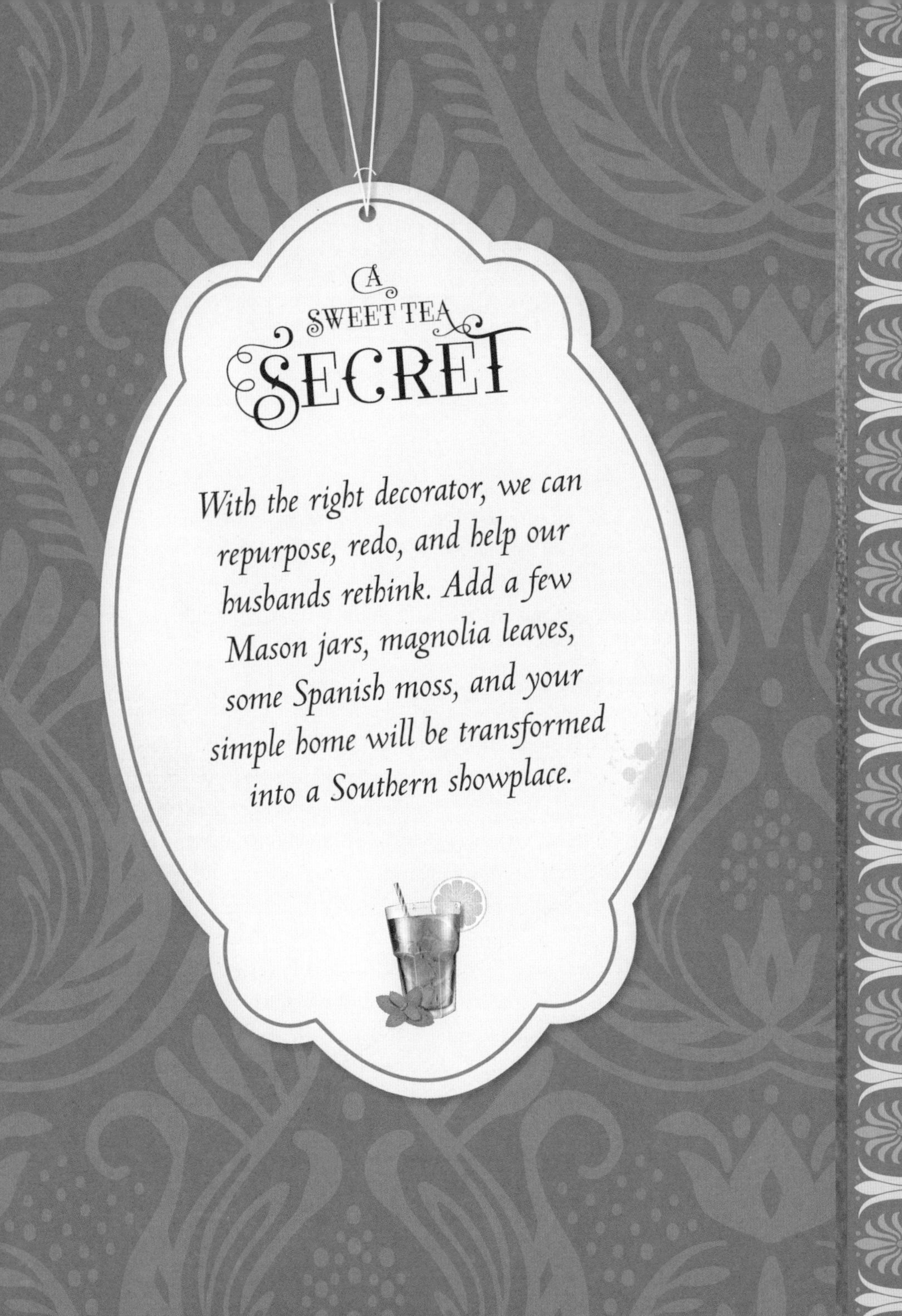

A Sweet Tea Secret

With the right decorator, we can repurpose, redo, and help our husbands rethink. Add a few Mason jars, magnolia leaves, some Spanish moss, and your simple home will be transformed into a Southern showplace.

26 WHITE SHOES, SMOCKED CLOTHES, AND BIG BOWS

IT'S THE DAY in a Southern mother's life that grieves her heart. The day you put off—you dare not mention it to friends—secretly praying you can change your husband's mind. You beg God to intervene, but your camo-wearing, gun-slingin' husband finally puts his foot down and transforms your family forever.

"You have got to stop dressing our boy like a girl," he demands. "It's embarrassing."

You mothers out there know what this edict means: No more white buck shoes, no more high white knee socks. Out go the smocked Jon Jon outfits. The days in your family when the heir to the throne dressed as Little Lord Fauntleroy are gone.

But if you have a younger daughter in the home, there is hope. At least there's hope as long as you can prevail against the pressure of counterculture and brand-identity stores that want to turn your precious little girl into someone who looks like a tramp-in-training.

One day my sweet Caroline and I walked into the iconic Eighty-Two Church boutique in downtown Charleston, where I bought my baby girl her first Charleston bonnet. Every well-bred Charleston child has one, although that headdress looks like a giant, ruffled organza lampshade with a bow on top. I could not wait to walk into that beloved store with my precious young daughter to buy her my favorite smocked dress, which featured Charleston's Rainbow Row on the bodice.

Then the unthinkable happened. Caroline spotted a pair of tight jeans and a cropped glittery top in another store window. What? On Church Street? Another Yankee vendor attempting to change our Southern ways. Caroline stared longingly at the garments and said, "Oh, Momma, I want to wear *those* clothes."

My response was swift. "Jesus will be sad." I'm not saying my reaction was fair, but sometimes a mother has to do what a mother has to do. I had to pull out the Big Guy at that moment. And when your baby girl is five, invoking God in any discussion is a perfectly acceptable response.

We left Eighty-Two Church with my baby girl's shopping bags filled with hair bows, smocked dresses, white tights, and of course a pair of white shoes. She even had her own pearl necklace. (In the South, we start our young wearing pearls as soon as possible; they need to learn early the weight of social manners, style, and tight shoes that hurt your feet.) But it is an absolute no to pierced ears. Pierced ears come way later—eighth grade or beyond, if you can swing it.

Anyway, not long after our trip to downtown Charleston, I got a call from Caroline's first-grade teacher. "Uh, Jane, does Caroline have any jeans? She was playing on the playground and got her pantaloons stuck in a tire, and the white apron that goes with the dress is soiled. Plus, we lost her navy blue bow that matches her dress."

You're asking me about jeans? Seriously? "Losing her bow," I said, "that's what you should be concerned about."

In the South, bows are essential. Big bows are a precursor to high hair. As we say in the South, the higher the bow, the closer one is to God. The bigger the bow the better, but when the Southern-belle-in-training reaches a certain age, the bows should be attached to a headband. It's more fashionable. But never under any circumstances should a proper young lady come home from first grade without her bow. It simply is not done.

Later I bought Caroline another bow. And I got her one of the most adorable outfits you can imagine: a farm-themed sweater with a barn door on the back. In class, one of those boys with cootie-fied hands teased her by opening the barn door until it would not latch anymore. She had had

enough. Caroline wheeled around in her desk and said to the intruder, "I don't know what you are looking for but there may be a mule behind that barn door, and one of us may give you a swift kick!" These are the times that make a Southern momma proud.

Body changes . . . wardrobe challenges and hormones. Little by little, we were approaching a time when my dear sweet Caroline's wardrobe would shift and fill and stretch in ways that would hurt my heart something terrible.

When that day arrived, my baby girl, who was always a compliant child, said, "Momma, how long do I have to wear a bow in my hair?"

"Caroline, you wear a bow until Code Red."

"Why then? Why can't I stop sooner?"

"Because it's hard to fit both feminine protection and a bow in your purse at the same time. Now let's not talk about it anymore."

Gracious, what's this world coming to? Stores tempting young women to dress like Myrtle Beach hussies by wearing tacky outfits that show undeveloped body parts—or worse, push identity crises with gender confusion. I swear, some days I'm convinced the best thing the North left us after Reconstruction was common sense.

So what are girls made of?

Sugar and spice and all things nice
Sweet tea kisses and Charleston red rice
Smocked dresses with bows,
White tights on her toes
And as soon as possible,
Learn tae kwon do.

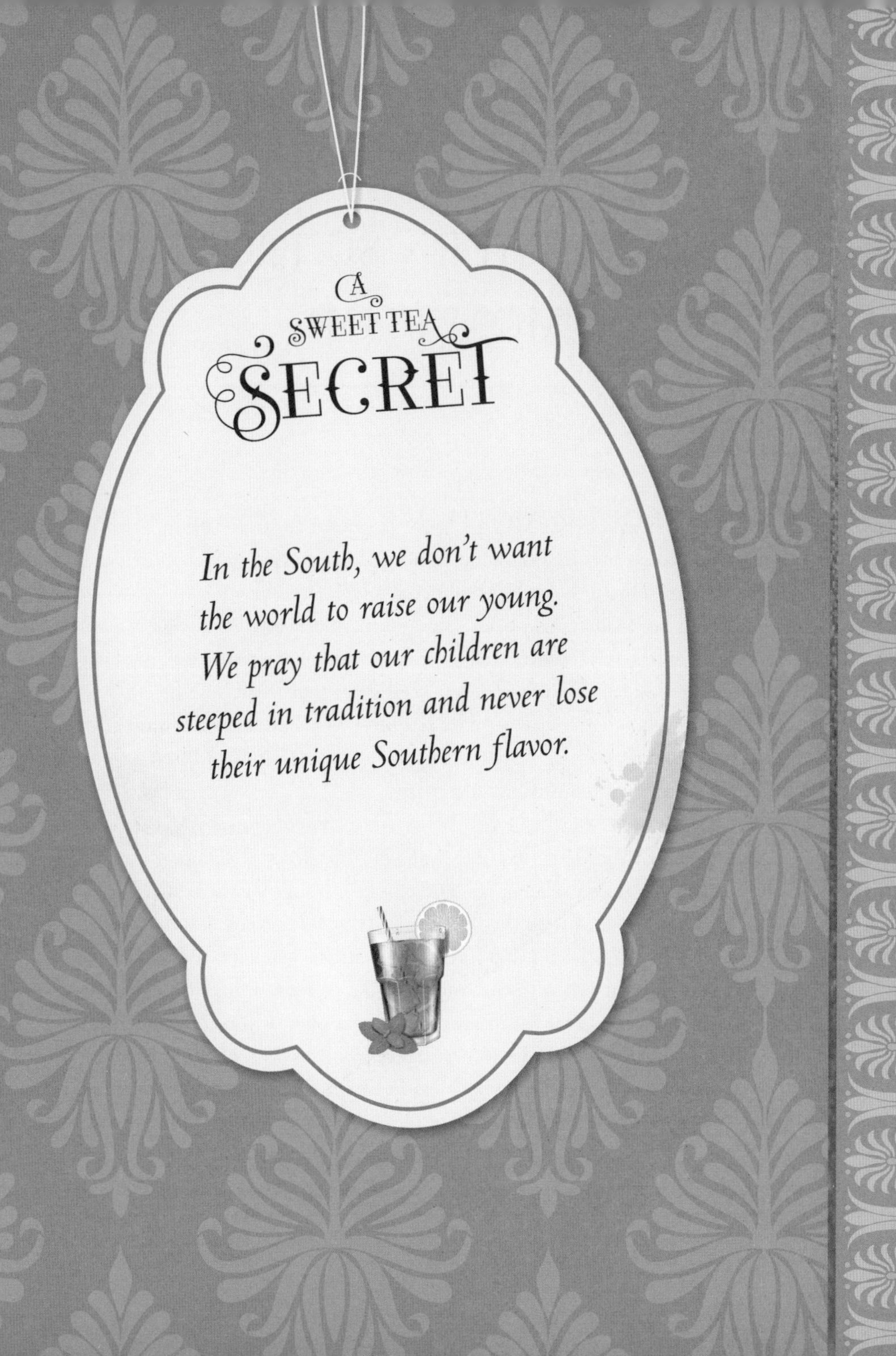

A Sweet Tea Secret

In the South, we don't want the world to raise our young. We pray that our children are steeped in tradition and never lose their unique Southern flavor.

27

SOUTHERN SCHOOL MOM FLOP

SINCE MY MOTHER was beautiful from top to bottom, and loads of fun, I desperately wanted her to be a room mother when I was in the first grade. I will never forget the look she gave me when I told her that she had been volunteered. It was my first experience with the blank stare. Eleanor lit her Kent menthol cigarette, took a long, ashy drag, and calmly replied, "Tell them that I will buy the ice."

Oh, what a wise woman! If only I had repeated this comment when my children were in elementary school—it would have saved lots of time, confusion, and energy.

It's just weird when a teacher who is twenty years younger than you are is suddenly in control of your life. They challenge your child's stress level and self-esteem, and can take hold of your home. My first experience with the tween teacher was when she asked parents to supply glue sticks. I had tons of glue sticks—*hot* glue sticks. That did not go over well with the teacher. I had to redeem myself.

When Easter rolled around, I had a plan. I would impress the tween teacher and the domestic diva mothers with an adorable bunny cake—made from scratch. I was in such a rush, I took the cake out of the oven half baked. I added icing and decorations to bring the bunny to life. It was a proud moment serving the children cake until one of the gooey bunny ears slid off the cake plate and fell splat on the floor. That was just the beginning of years of not fitting in as the Southern school mom.

I studied those perfectly coiffured Southern women every morning. Their favorite thing to do was exit their beautiful SUVs and walk their children into the school. For safety reasons? Oh, no. It was the morning walk down the fashion runway. I swear I saw one of those monogrammed divas with matching outfits turn and pose for the rest of us to see her and her twin spawn. The Show resembled New York City's Fashion Week. And all of the other moms did the same thing. Depending on the season, everything was themed—sweaters decorated with fall leaves and matching shoes. Christmas was the worst themed fashion statement—reindeer antlers decorated their heads, electric sweaters that blink worn over leggings with red candy canes.

Southerners historically like themes. My friend Dixie, who is anti-theme, moved into a new neighborhood. It was October and I knew she was in trouble when most of the folks on her street decorated with pumpkins, cornstalks, and stuffed scarecrows in their yards. I had to have the *talk*.

"Dixie," I said in a firm voice. "Your neighbors are themed, and if you want to fit in, you have to do something so they will know you are one of them."

It was a hard discussion to have since I needed to take my own advice. I have to give Dixie a shout-out. She did her best to blend, but it was painful.

And speaking of painful, after a period of time, your children will reminisce and make fun of you. My children love to tell the story of how Thomas and I acted and dressed when we drove them to school. Now, I can see the school from my house, but when I drove the children we were late most of the time. Thomas, in his beautiful Brooks Brothers suit, would drive the children to school a half hour ahead of time, put the car in park, pray with them, and conclude with "Children, be followers of God, not of man."

Here are my children's recollections of when I drove them to school.

Holmes: "You would yell and tell us to hurry up, we were late. Then put on your sunglasses and winter coat even if it was 90 degrees and race to school drinking a cup of coffee." (That was

correct; I was trying to hide my leave-me-alone stained pajamas underneath the coat.)

To continue . . .

"When we got to the school, instead of praying and sharing motivational/Jesus tidbits, you yelled, 'Run!'"

Caroline: "Wednesdays were the worst. We were late and the school children were holding hands and praying at Meet Me at the Pole. You would also say, 'Break into that circle and act like you've been there.'"

Then Caroline tearfully added, "I hope God has mercy on our souls."

Caroline tends to be dramatic at times.

Okay, so I did not blend, fit in, or theme. And as the years passed, I learned to quote my wonderful, beautiful fun mother and say, "I'll buy the ice."

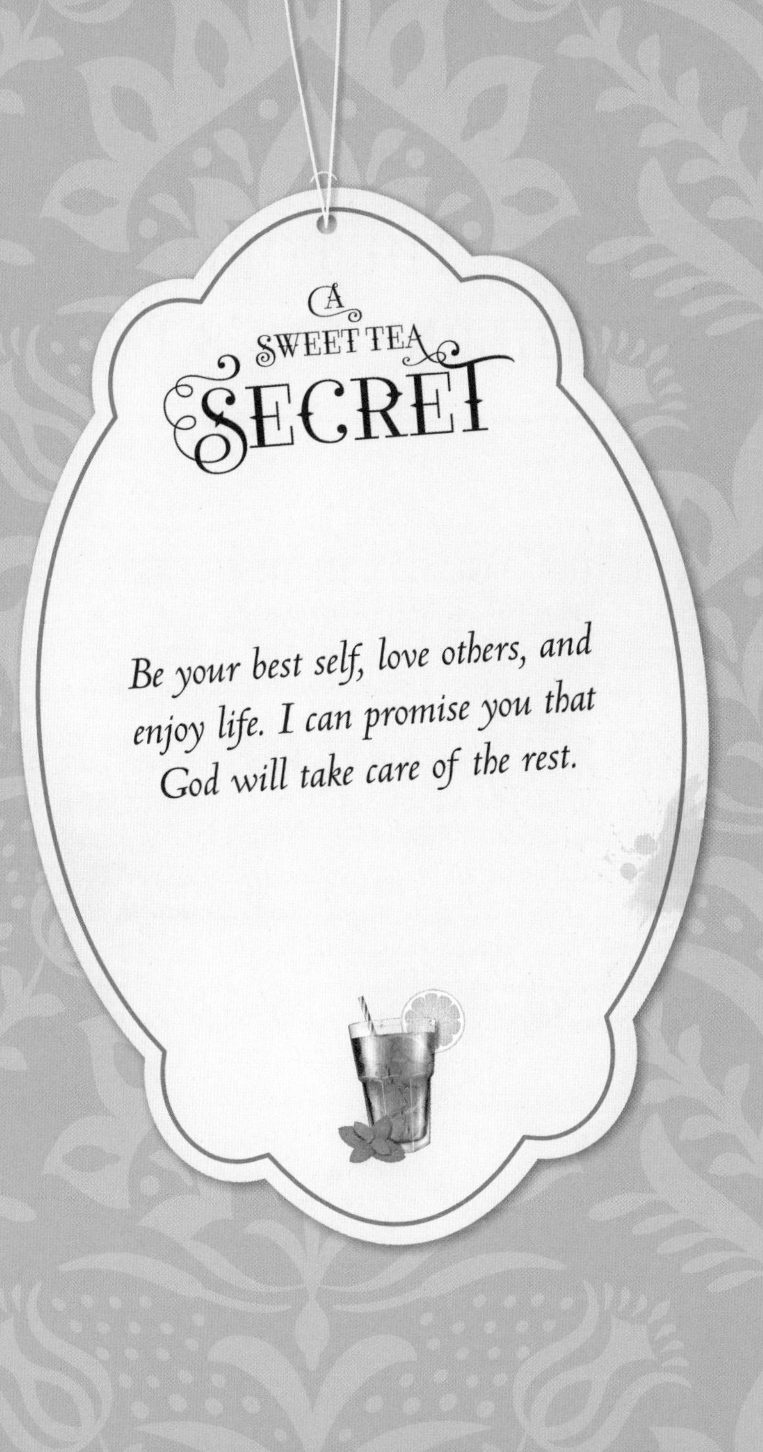
A
SWEET TEA
SECRET
Be your best self, love others, and enjoy life. I can promise you that God will take care of the rest.

28

PRISSY THE PORKER: A SOUTHERN GENT'S TALE

AT TIMES, YOU CAN HEAR TOO much information during intercessory prayer in Sunday school. But when it comes to a Southern boy loving his momma, nothing is off limits.

"Wellll . . ." said Dan in his Southern drawl, "y'all pray for Momma. She's having back surgery this week."

"Yep. Gonna slice her open, peel back her skin, and . . . after that I'm not sure what happens. Doctors said something about exposed nerves and discs and 'bout there being a slight chance of paralysis. If y'all don't mind, how about praying for me, too? It's gonna be rough."

"We will," I said to Dan, trying to sound sympathetic. "It's your momma, and I know you are concerned."

"Well, mostly I'm worried 'bout her cat, Prissy. Vet's been telling Momma that her cat's too fat, so I'm putting Prissy on a diet. Only exercise that cat gets is moving her head from the feeding bowl to the water bowl. Prissy's a porker."

None of us said it out loud, but a few of us women were probably thinking, *If Dan is willing to fat-shame his momma's cat, what's he saying about me behind my back?*

"Dumb cat is so fat it cannot lick after itself," Dan kept on as if unaware that we didn't want to hear about his momma's cat's hygiene issues. "Momma asked me to help that cat . . . you know, wipe. I tried, but the darn thing hissed at me 'cause this is what cats do when you irritate them. But that cat irritates me since I did get a good-enough look to know that she was needing some hygiene help, if you get my drift. So I got me a spray bottle and a wet paper towel, held up her tail, and—"

"We'll pray for your momma," I said. "And her cat. And you."

And I meant it, though mostly I meant I would pray that the good Lord Jesus would help Dan know when enough information becomes too much information.

The next week Dan entered Sunday school with a smile. We couldn't wait to hear how his momma's surgery went and if Prissy the Porker had lost pounds.

"Momma's doing great, thanks for asking."

"And the cat?" I have to admit, the kitty was on my mind a lot that week. I guess it's just how I'm wired.

"Back to licking."

Before Dan could continue, we gave thanks to Jesus and quickly moved on to a passage about caring for your neighbor.

If you're looking for a sweet tea Southern secret from this story, it's this: There are some things you can't make up or clean up and are best not mentioned in polite or even impolite company. Anything south of your belly button falls into this DMZ (Don't Mention Zone), even when it involves your momma and her beloved pets.

Actually, there is another cat tale here. Prissy porked right back up and eventually went to her reward of unlimited kitty cuisine in the sky. Dan's momma decided to get another cat and appropriately named her Hissy.

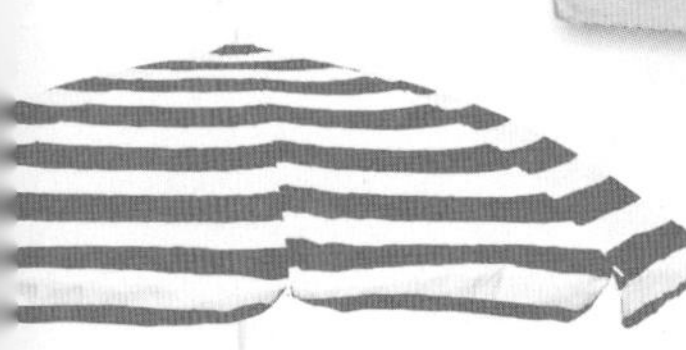

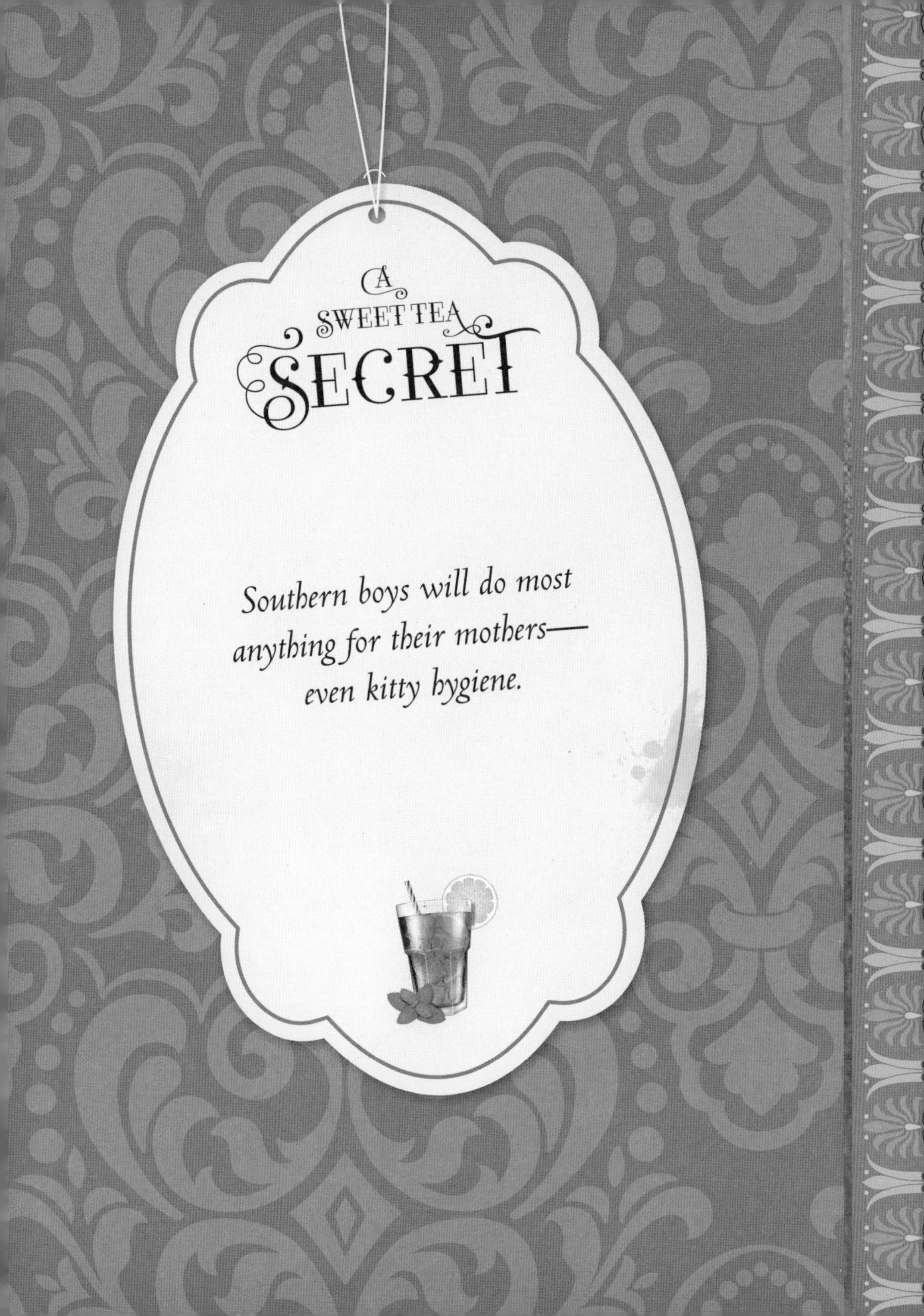
A
SWEET TEA
SECRET
Southern boys will do most
anything for their mothers—
even kitty hygiene.

PART VI

Sacred Southern Traditions

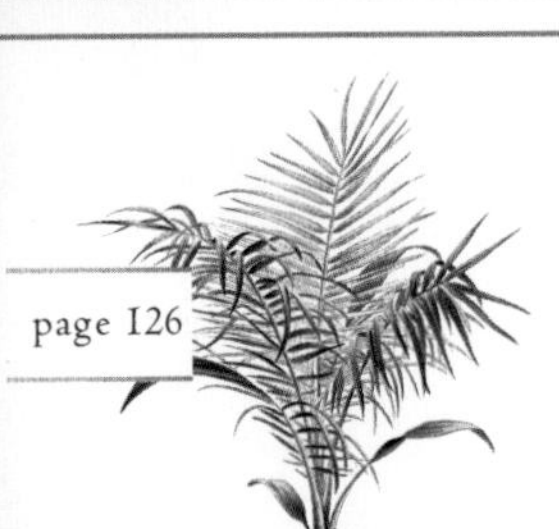

29

SOCIAL GRACES

HER NAME WAS MRS. WHALEY, and most of Charleston society waited breathlessly to receive her letter—the one that would change the course of their at-age child's future. Mrs. Whaley was famous. You may own one of her books, maybe *Mrs. Whaley Entertains* or *Mrs. Whaley's Charleston Kitchen*. As I was researching her books, I noticed at the time that *Mrs. Whaley and Her Charleston Garden* ranked in the top one hundred books in the "Gardening & Horticulture Essays" category on Amazon. Every well-bred Charlestonian has an arsenal of Mrs. Whaley books, one to display and others to give as gifts.

Years ago, young men and women danced, bowed, and curtsied every Wednesday night in Charleston's South Carolina Hall. But mostly they learned Southern manners. The connections they made could be the difference between marrying someone South of Broad or someone from another, less desirable part of the county. And God forbid your child marry a "two *m*" Simmons.

I once heard a woman introduce herself to another in her clique this way: "I live on Legare Street, and I am Mrs. Simons . . . *one m*." I never found out why she made sure people knew her last name was spelled with one m. Maybe one of her kin embarrassed the family, so they decided to change the spelling. You never know with the downtown Charleston crowd.

And yes, we Jenkins girls received the invitation from Mrs. Whaley; however, our mother would not drive us into town on Wednesday nights since she was busy being domestic. Regardless, there is never ever an excuse for failing to learn our Southern social graces. Social graces open doors and close them. They build bonds between families and friends in ways that rival blood relations. Social graces are the threads that stitch together the fabric of Southern culture.

My growing-up-best-friend, Emily, went to cotillion on Wednesday nights at the South Carolina Hall. Since Momma refused to drive my sister and me into town on those evenings, Emily was kind enough to teach me the foxtrot and other important dances. In fact, Emily reenacted the entire Wednesday night experience for me so I could become a viable candidate for Charleston society. Had it not been for Emily, I might never have been allowed to date Porter-Gaud prep-school boys, and to this day I'm grateful.

Miss Martha was our very own Johns Island version of Mrs. Whaley. Miss Martha gave us our first piece of silver and taught us to never send a thank-you note with the words *thank you* on the front. As Miss Martha explained, sending a thank-you note with *thank you* written on the front means the thanker does not know how to thank properly. Acceptable stationery is ivory, with a raised monogram printed on 110-pound card stock. I've witnessed older Southern women open an envelope and give the invitation the ultimate test of approval. They hold the stationery up to the light to locate the watermark of excellence—*Crane.* The mark dictates both the quality of gift given and the amount of money spent.

Engraved stationery is always preferred, but thermography is accepted. Thermography printing involves mixing ink with plastic and hoping it doesn't chip off over time; engraving permanently marks the paper. If you care about your reputation, send your best.

Most, if not all, Bible teaching can be summarized in two rules: Love God and love your neighbor. Southern social graces can be condensed into one command: Do not be tacky.

Tacky is the go-to word in the South. It's an adjective, noun, verb, pronoun, adverb, and expletive. It is the one-word label that will doom your social future and curse your offspring for generations to come. No amount of Ajax (remember that product?) can scrub off the tacky curse.

When I was growing up, Ajax was the mother ship of cleansers, used to remove everything. But nothing, absolutely nothing can remove tacky. Tacky is like that tattoo you got that now stretches and sags when your rolls and cellulite lumps expand. Tacky shows a lack of good taste (and, as Miss Martha would say, good sense). Tacky is cheap showiness that reflects a lack of good breeding. The absolute worst part of tacky is the way it sticks. If someone tacky calls another person tacky, the accusation "she's tacky" completely cancels her tackiness. That's how ticky-tacky tacky is. Southern women, regardless of their station in life, understand and avoid this label until the day they draw their last breath.

You may have heard that when older folks get dementia, the last thing to go is music. I totally disagree. I know for a fact, it is having a clear understanding of what's tacky. One of my dearest friends was living in a nursing home. The severity of her dementia was very upsetting. She was our resident expert on the proper use of the English language. Because she wasn't communicating anymore, we sat for at least an hour in silence. I then decided to take her into the large sitting area, where the staff held various activities for the residents.

I watched a very sweet Southern woman enter the room and sit at the upright piano. "Okay, ya'll," she said in her perky drawl, "we are gonna sing some good ol', toe-tappin' gospel songs. But I cannot seem to find my songbook. I wonder where my hymnal is at."

Suddenly, my dear mute friend perked up and repeated her English lesson: Never end a sentence with a preposition. In her soft Southern voice I heard, "It's behind the *a* and the *t*."

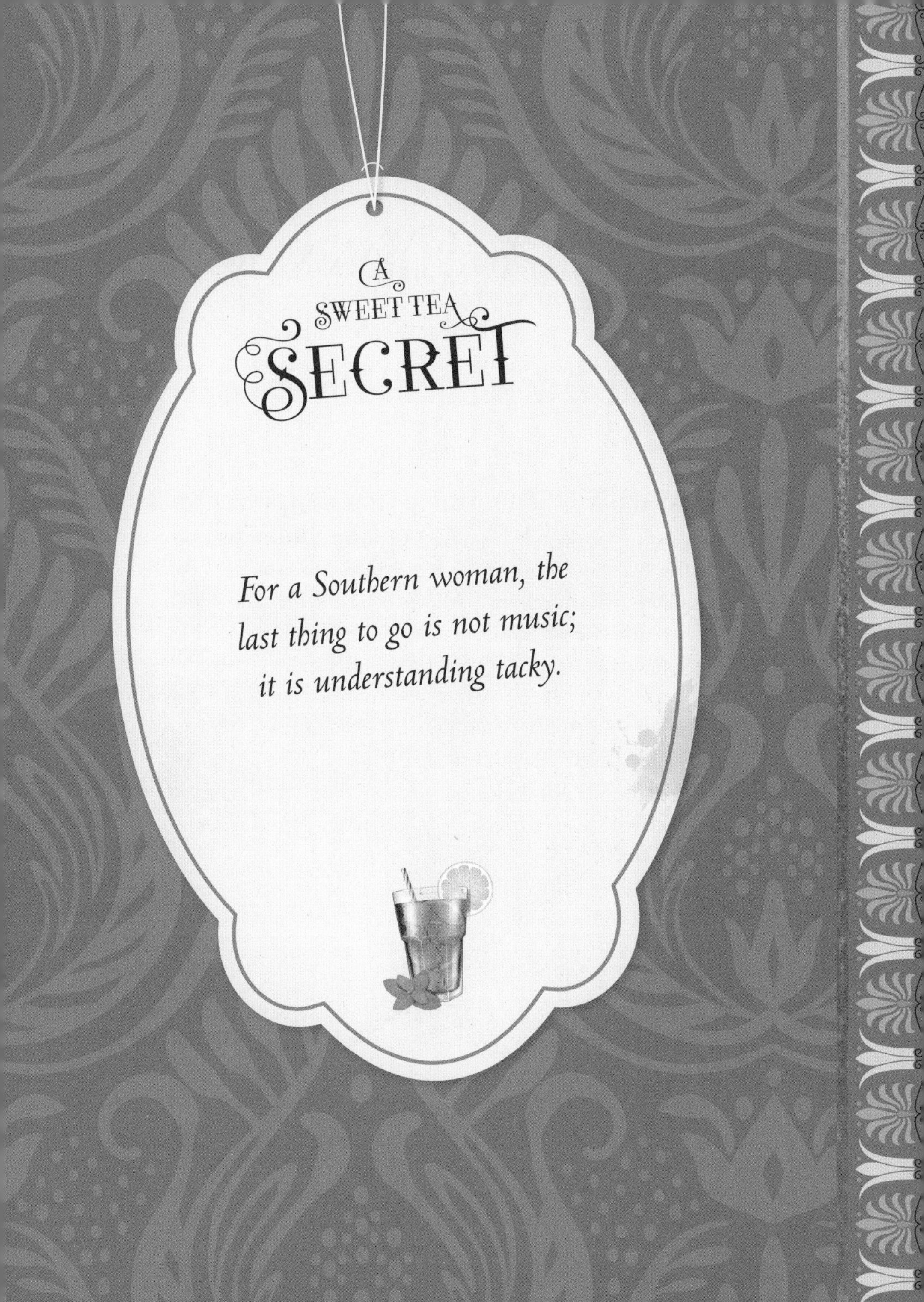
A
SWEET TEA
SECRET
For a Southern woman, the
last thing to go is not music;
it is understanding tacky.

30

Magical Manners

IMAGINE YOU ARE gathered around the Thanksgiving table with your extended family. All eyes are fixed on your precious toddler. Someone looks at this blessed boy and asks, "Do you like Grandma's mac and cheese?" This sweet, adorable child with his golden curls, the one who will carry on the family name, offers the absolute worst response: "Yes."

Forks drop. All eyes shift to you and your husband. There is a stunned silence. You are fully aware of the enormous infraction and say to your child, "Honey, yes what?"

The blessed boy is clueless.

"Sweetie," you continue, "say, 'yes ma'am.'" And so begins the training and retraining in Southern manners.

Years later, after this same child is all grown up and has become a polite, polished Southern gentleman, he lands an interview for a fabulous job up *Nawth*. He is seated in the company boardroom, having lunch with the top executives and the female CEO. She asks this Southern gentleman, "Did you tour the office?"

"Yes, ma'am. Impressive."

Forks drop. All eyes fixate on him. Stunned silence reminds him once more that he's a stranger in a strange land.

"What did you call me?" asks the offended CEO.

Now comes the time a Southern momma has been waiting for—the moment that will reveal whether the child fully understands how Southerners can be both gracious and proud at the same time.

"Well, ma'am, in the South we're raised to respect those in authority, stand when our elders enter a room, stand when a woman comes to the table, offer to help women—or really anyone—lift items that seem too heavy. We say *ma'am* and *sir* out of respect, because we know those who are in charge are there for a reason. Sometimes if we're not careful, we'll get caught saying grace before meals."

Southerners understand that not everyone appreciates being called out with politeness and respect. A good many would rather that their tough, hard-nosed business persona be gender-neutral. But in the South, we make distinctions between genders, age, physical strength, and mental aptitude. We see *people,* not simply *groups.* If someone needs help or has earned respect, we give it. Not every Southerner, of course. But in general we live by God's Golden Rule: Do for others what you wish they would do for you.

Turns out that boy was hired despite his manners, and the CEO's daughter fell madly in love with him. She figured a man who will stay true to his convictions and upbringing would stay true to her. Years later, he took over the family business and moved his family back home to his parents' place on the Charleston Battery.

We may not all look the same or have the same history, culture, or beliefs . . . but we can all be polite and respectful. That's not just a Southern thing; it's a people thing.

The best folks are those who stay true to their upbringing. They practice good manners and delightful charm. Celebrate your uniqueness and don't bow to the pressure of changing into a homogenized clone.

31 Why Aunt Binny Had a Dead Chicken on Her Ceiling

SOUTHERN MOTHERS HAVE several "talks" with their daughters: the monthly cycle, sex (mainly how to avoid it), what boys want all the time (sex), how to avoid boys, how to poke a boy on the head when he won't take no for an answer, and how to use a pressure cooker.

I was informed that only the best cooks could conquer the pressure cooker. The key is a proper fear of the "little man" dancing on the top of the cooker balanced with the knowledge of what happens when you decide your recipe is ready as opposed to the pressure cooker's little man making the decision. Momma and Tootsie warned me for years.

"Ja-un," Momma warned, "this is a very dangerous machine."

Then Tootsie chimed in. "You blow up dis kitchen if you don' know what you doin."

My mother always concluded the lecture this way: "One time, your aunt Binny had to scrape a chicken off her ceiling."

This is what we do as Southern women. As challenging as it may sound, we pass down pressure-cooker stories. Our young must be taught about the thrill of the outcome as well as respect for the art of high-pressure cooking. Now, I'm aware that there are other cookers on the market, but a Southern woman must master the mother ship of cookers: The Pot.

After years of trial and (mostly) error, I mastered the machine. Dining on my pressure-cooker-fabulous glazed-chicken entrée, my sweet Caroline said, "Oh, Momma, this is delicious! How did you make it?"

My Southern heritage kicked in and I just *had* to continue the tradition. "Caroline, this is a very dangerous machine. One time, your great-aunt Binny had to scrape a chicken off her ceiling."

That began a lengthy discussion about the monthly cycle, sex (mainly how to avoid it), what boys want all the time (sex), how to avoid boys, how to aim pepper spray when he won't take no for an answer, and the dangers of using a pressure cooker. And to watch out for the little man dancing.

"Mother, I'm married and almost thirty. I know all about sex, so is this about a pressure cooker, and is the little man dancing supposed to be a 2.0 version of the birds and the bees?"

For me, those mother-daughter talks stopped the day my mother passed away, and to be honest, I'd give almost anything to hear that lecture one more time.

I don't care how old you are or how many times you give instruction to your young'uns. Southern women still find a way to tell the same story over and over, even using the pressure cooker when necessary.

32

Sitting at the Southern "Churin' Table"

IT WAS A Jenkins family tradition—practically every holiday we journeyed to my grandparents' home on Johns Island for the family get-together. My immediate family only had a short drive down a dirt road; other family members drove for hours.

The young'uns were excited because we knew that all of us cousins would sit together. At first, we felt somewhat insulted since we longed to be grown-ups and have the honor of sitting with the adults. We did not realize how lucky we were to be sitting at our special table.

At the kid table, no one told you what to eat or how to eat. You could help yourself to a mountain of mac and cheese or Charleston red rice coated in bacon grease and nix the collards. You were free to lob a roll across the table or catapult green beans with your spoon.

Cholesterol? No one knew what it was.

Drumsticks were fried in Crisco, and we loved drinking our diabetes-inducing sweet tea. Chocolate delight, pecan pie, and an endless supply of benne-seed cookies were displayed all day on the sideboard.

No manners were required at the kid table. You could laugh out loud at that crazy cousin with your mouth wide open until co-cola or sweet tea escaped out your nose. You didn't have to clean your plate or listen to the proverbial lecture on starving children.

We should have known the adults were not happy sitting at the big table. Their conversations were guarded and boring. Some of the relatives didn't like each other and fantasized about starting a food fight. Many of the women ate salads that resembled the food on the bottom of hamster cages. They talked about the latest diet and slipped in a few condescending remarks about some of the food. Other aunts quietly prayed that their churin' at the kid table were behaving themselves. The men talked about football and how expensive things were. You could practically hear the stress in their voices.

Not at the kid table. We did not have a care in the world, and we had the time of our lives.

The adult table had china; the kids had Chinet. The adult plates were handled with care. The kids' plates were Frisbees before, after, and sometimes during the meal. The adult table was decorated with heirloom flatware and Great-Grandmother's handmade tablecloth. The kid table was a card table adorned with plastic utensils and Solo cups. Our napkins were paper towels—perfect for food fights.

The adults could not eat their favorite foods. We all felt sorry for our parents, aunts, and uncles. We sometimes slipped them the good stuff under the table. Strange how eating turkey made the adults go to sleep while the same meat made us run around the yard.

So relish (could not help myself) the memories of carefree days at the kid table. Those occasions may be some of your best memories as an adult. When we gather to celebrate the lives of our aunts, uncles, parents, and cousins, there will be endless servings of stories laced with unforgettable love and laughter.

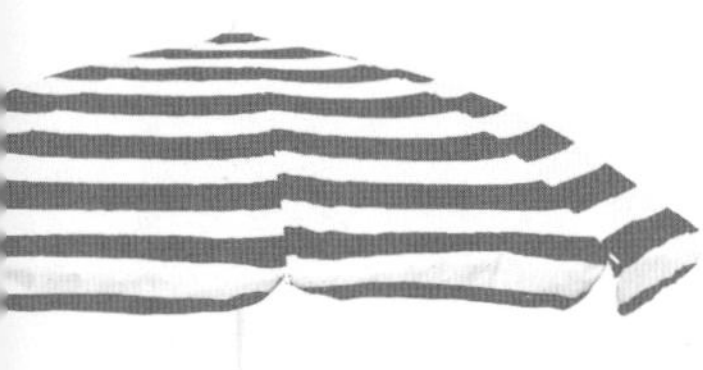

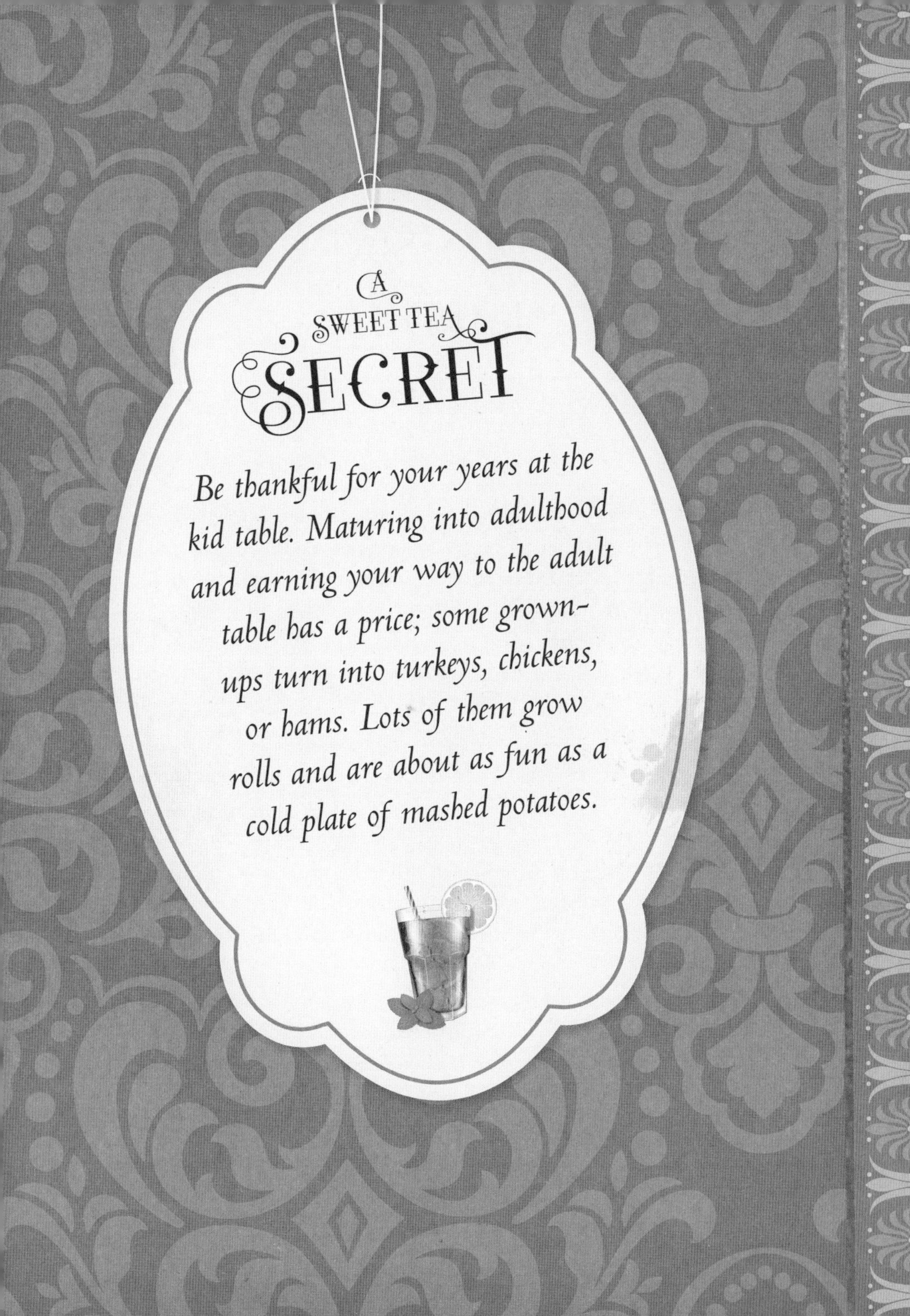
A SWEET TEA SECRET
Be thankful for your years at the
kid table. Maturing into adulthood
and earning your way to the adult
table has a price; some grown-
ups turn into turkeys, chickens,
or hams. Lots of them grow
rolls and are about as fun as a
cold plate of mashed potatoes.

33

DADDY'S NEW HAIRDO

IT WAS ONE of the best Christmas gifts ever. My sister and I loved watching Momma's beautician style her hair. So what better gift than a Maddie Mod Deadstock Mannequin hairdo doll, complete with rollers, brush, hair products, and even a carrying case? Momma believed my sister and I should be fully educated in the fine art of fabulous hair and makeup. After all, we were Southern girls in training. We rolled Maddie Mod's hair, back-combed it, added the hair extension, and topped off the plastic diva's do with the all-important pink ribbon. In a matter of weeks, we were professional hairdressers.

Every day at noon, Daddy would come in from the farm and eat a large meal. Then he would crash in his pleather recliner, and in a matter of minutes he was, as Momma would say, at Lily White's party. Not long after he stretched out in that recliner, the snoring began.

With Daddy sawing logs in a deep sleep, my sister and I had a brilliant idea. Since we had mastered the Maddie Mod head, we needed a new challenge: Daddy's not-so-mod head. Maddie Mod was easy since the mannequin had lots of long hair, but Daddy's hair was not so easy—he had a patch on top of his head and hair on the sides. Very carefully, we separated each section and began our beauty magic.

We managed to roll the top and the sides using every one of those small pink rollers. We were so proud of our creation, we decided to top it off by spraying his hair with Momma's Breck hair-setting spray. We thought the sound of the spewing aerosol can would wake him, but since he was treating and spraying ditch banks, it probably sounded normal. To complete our creation, we mischievously topped off Daddy's do with the Maddie Mod hair extension.

Like typical children, we moved on to the next activity. In the meantime, Daddy woke up, put on his cap, and off he went to a tractor supply place to pick up some parts. Upon entering the store, Daddy did what most Southern gentlemen do—he removed his hat. Seeing Daddy's hair coiffed with pink miniature rollers and a red hair extension, everyone in view burst out laughing, the kind of laughter that makes you snort. The tractor supply folks could not pull themselves together to tell him what was so funny; they just pointed and laughed.

Daddy headed to the men's room, where he saw what was making the guys convulse into snorts. But it got worse. Remember that Breck hair-setting spray? It did its job. When Daddy removed the rollers, his hair resembled Bozo the clown. In fact, to give it a modern-day comparison, his hair was styled into a high-top 'fro. And honey, his hair was set; a shower was the only hope to calm it.

I remember that day like it was yesterday. What sticks in my mind is how much it made my father laugh and how he told that story over and over again. Farming is a very stressful profession, and with only a small window of time to earn a living from the "money crop" of tomatoes, laughter and fun were not visitors in our home very often.

But Daddy taught me some lessons that day: Be able to laugh at yourself and try to find the humor in everyday experiences. I guess you can say it was a hair-raising experience (can't help myself) filled with fun, laughter, and a story that continues to be told.

Daddy left us in 1996 when his heart quit beating—ironically, while he was in his recliner. I can't wait to throw my arms around his neck and hear that story one more time.

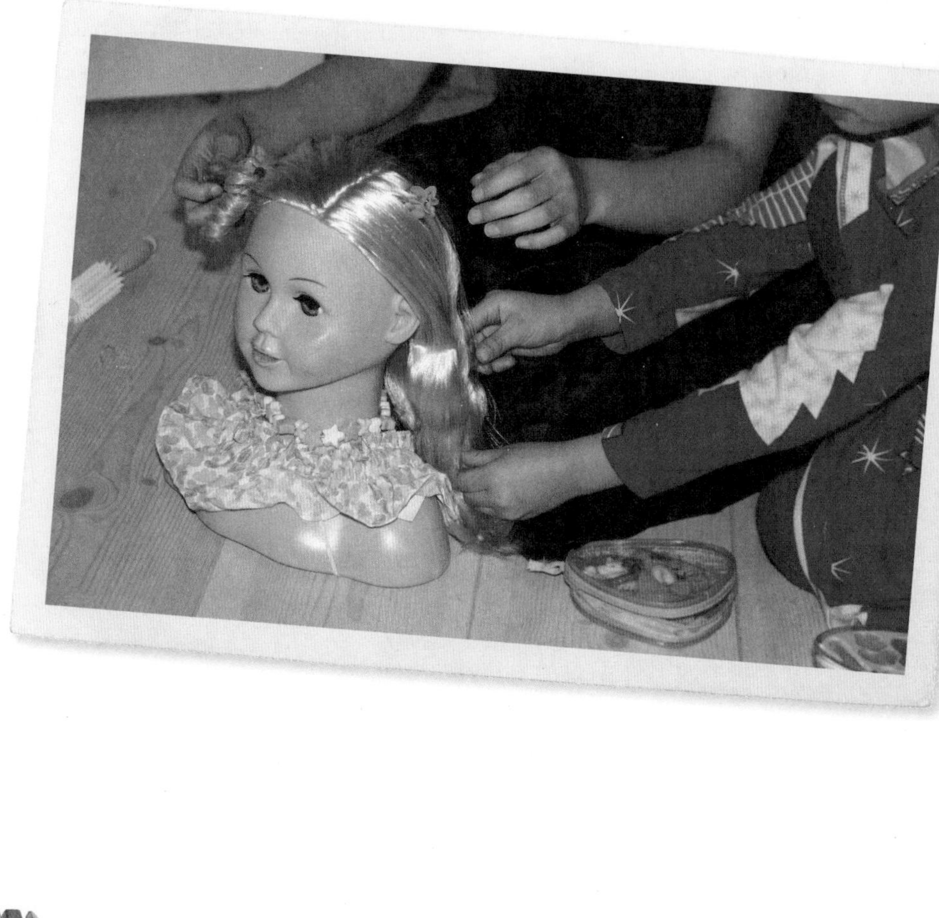

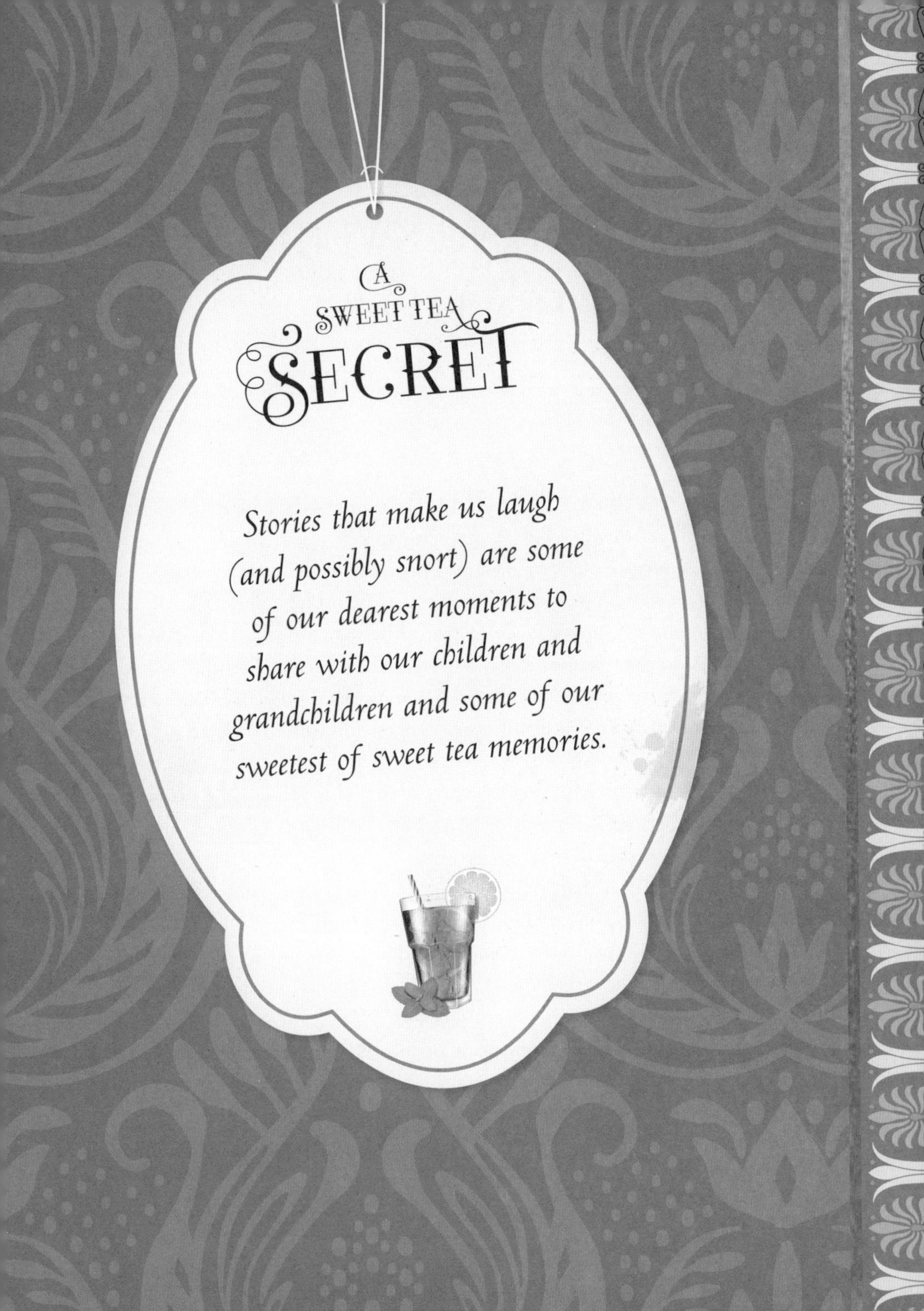

A Sweet Tea Secret

Stories that make us laugh (and possibly snort) are some of our dearest moments to share with our children and grandchildren and some of our sweetest of sweet tea memories.

34

Telling Sweet Tea Tales

IT WAS WEDNESDAY morning—the hallowed hair day at Belks back when Belk ended with an *s*.

Seated in our family's aqua Pontiac with the hard white top, Momma and I waited for the store to open. The Pontiac's small triangular window was wide open while she tapped her manicured nails on the steering wheel. With her elbow propped on the armrest, wearing her rhinestoned, wing-tipped sunglasses, Momma commented on practically every person who walked in front of our car.

"Look at that sweet woman holding that young child's hand. Her daughter is not raising that child. That dear grandmother had to take over."

"You hear that?" Momma asked. "He has taps on his shoes. Bet he is married and has a girlfriend. Disgusting."

She bumped open the vent window a little more. "Oh, would you look at how that woman is dressed? She needs a mirror and a good friend."

I was amazed at how many people Momma knew, though in reality she was making up stories. She did not know a soul who walked past the car. But sitting with Momma in her Pontiac while her imagination ran on and on about strangers was an early version of reality-show entertainment for me.

Some twenty years later, my daughter, Caroline, sat in the car with me as we waited for Hobby Lobby to open. Suddenly, I found myself saying, "Look at that sweet woman holding that young child's hand. You know her disrespectful daughter is not raising that child."

Call it what you want . . . weird, funny, or off-the-wall . . . but in the South we call it conversational storytelling. We love our tales and pass them down from generation to generation. Some are true; some are almost true. Many are based on shoddy memories. A few are outright lies that we think happened 'cause we've told them so often. It's a privileged art in the South to spin a good story to pass the time or reinforce a lesson using people, places, . . . or even an overheated dog.

Momma once used the example of our dog to explain to my sister and me about how babies are made. Our sweet Honey constantly had a pack of up-to-no-good dogs following her around in our yard.

Looking out of the back door, Momma yelled, "You see that! Look at how popular Honey is with all those mutts. I want you girls to remember how many friends Honey has now. But let me tell you, in a few weeks, no one will be her friend. Soon she will be taking care of yapping mutts. No fun trips to the beach with friends; no more going to the mall. Girls, don't be like our moral-less dog, Honey, waggling your tail. I raised you better than that, and I hope you remember it."

Even when my sister and I started dating, Momma spoke that last sentence as both a reminder and warning: "Have a good time, but be a lady, Honey."

God bless our bleached-blonde dog.

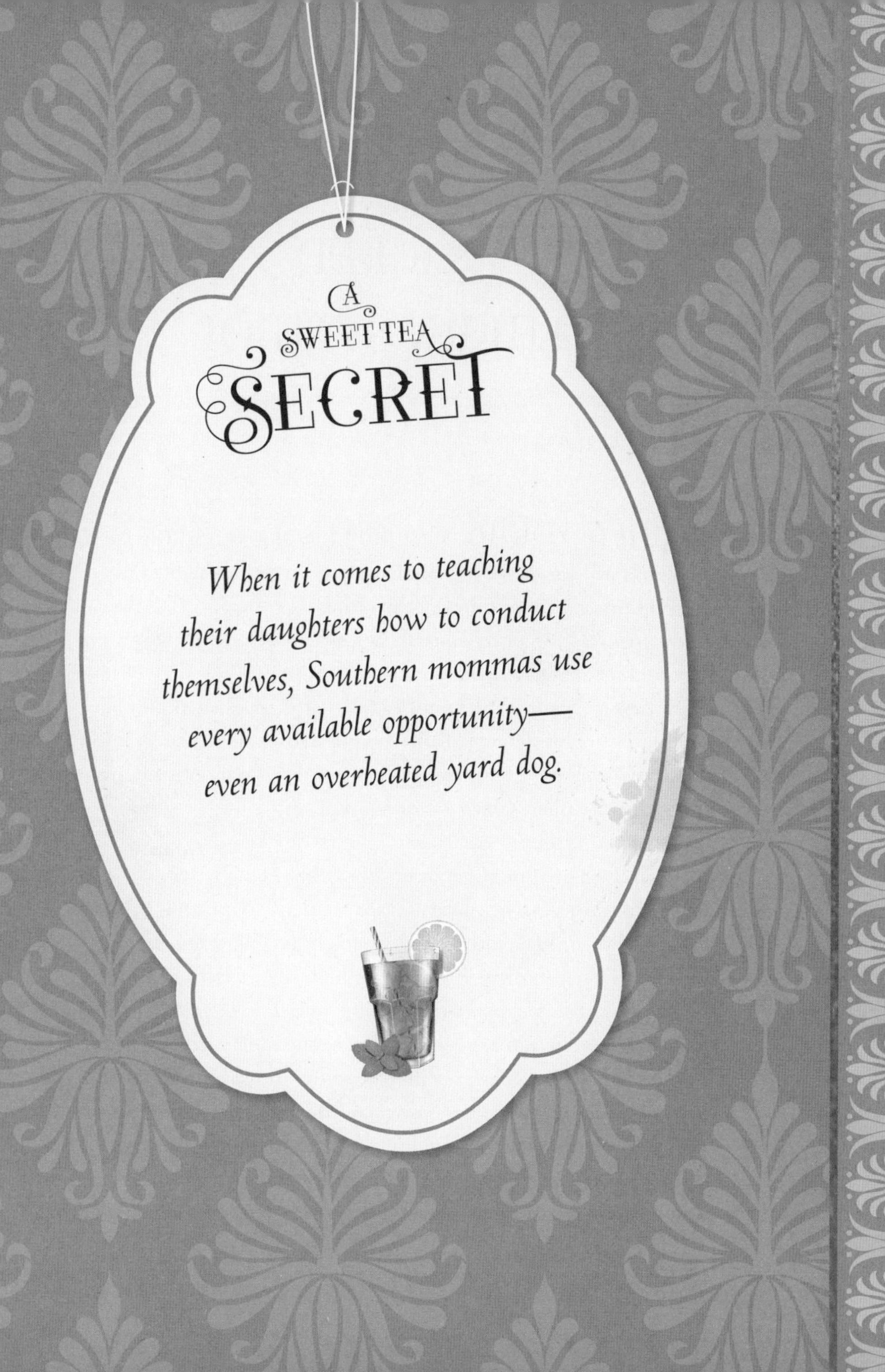

A Sweet Tea Secret

When it comes to teaching their daughters how to conduct themselves, Southern mommas use every available opportunity—even an overheated yard dog.

page 150

35

A Sacred Southern Symbol

WHEN YOU'RE CAUGHT in slow traffic, you see them stuck on back windshields. You may sleep on one at night. They show up on bathroom towels, beach tote bags, men's cuffs, silverware, pillow shams, and pocket squares. You may have one hanging around your neck or dangling from your ears right now. They cling to shoes and sometimes will sit on your head. What is this sacred Southern symbol that helps define you? If you guessed palmetto bugs, I don't blame you. Palmetto bugs are another Southern symbol, although we don't consider them sacred—just a nuisance.

I'm talking about *monograms.*

I received my first monogram as a Christmas gift: an engraved locket, given to me when I turned sixteen. In a script font, of course, with my three initials interlocked. It was beautiful, original . . . it was all me. That same year one of my high school friends also got a locket for Christmas; hers only had one initial. Like close friends will do, I pretended it was as special as mine, but I felt sorry for her.

One of my Southern sistahs shared her monogram story of being at a pharmacy in the Midwest. Unfortunately, she didn't have a second form of identification. In a clever move, she hoisted her purse so the pharmacist could see her four monogrammed initials. With her big smile and drawl, she convinced the pharmacist that, in the South, a monogram is considered a legal form of identification in many places. The trick worked for my Southern sistah. She got her prescription.

In the South, we engrave or monogram almost everything. Maybe it is an indelible, undeniable proof of ownership that goes way back to the War of Northern Aggression, when our treasures were seized by Yankees. It may take more than a hundred years, but our mission is to track down our possessions. Payback is an inevitable part of history; although our land is still being taken, the price tag is much higher.

When I got married, my silver pattern was Fairfax. If you are a born-and-reared Charlestonian, it is built into your DNA that you transport all your silver to Litaker's that was located on King Street in downtown Charleston for engraving. And not just any engraving . . . it must be done by hand.

I guess you could say that monograms and engravings are the original Southern version of the microchip. One thing's for sure: The time-honored practice of marking our treasures helps Southerners track down family heirlooms in thrift shops and antique stores all over the country.

JHJ

You may find some of your family's treasures in faraway places. Bring them home and make sure your heirs know the story behind each one.

36

The Secret Family Recipe

Before I moved to the quaint community of Johnston, South Carolina, my friend Mary told me a story that is hard to forget and speaks volumes about our Southern matriarchs.

Mary was new to our small town, and as Southern folk will do, an older, more established woman in the community called on her. Opening her front door, Mary was surprised to be greeted by a chauffeur in formal attire. The chauffeur proceeded to present Mary with a hot pecan (pronounced pee-can, *not* pe-caun) pie.

A shiny, late-model Cadillac (complete with winged fins) was parked in Mary's driveway, which signified the grand arrival of some prominent dignitary. In the Cadillac's back seat sat her caller, Johnston's own Grand Dame. It was a scene right out of *Driving Miss Daisy*. Mary noticed a gloved hand waving and decided to approach the car to show her appreciation, but she quickly got the message that a simple wave was adequate.

Several days later, Mary called the Grand Dame to thank her for the delicious pecan pie. After complimenting the woman on her pie, Mary said, "I would love your recipe."

Silence.

Then Mary heard, "Why, dah'lin we never share ow-ah sacred recipes. This has been a family secret for ye-ahs. I would never give anyone outside of the family the list of ingredients."

So many thoughts ran through poor Mary's brain. She didn't have a clue about the proper way to respond to a gift from the Grand Dame of a small Southern town. Would this faux pas tarnish her reputation? Would this mistake lead to Mary's excommunication from Johnston? Not that we're Charleston. Lawd, we're whole stratospheres beneath that mantle of social upper crust. But so many of our small Southern towns have unspoken rules that need to be followed. God forbid that you become a topic of discussion at the local Piggly Wiggly. Embarrassed, Mary called a family member for consolation.

"Say what?" Her stunned mother-in-law about choked on her dentures. "That prissy pants knows better. That pecan pie recipe is on page 244 in the *Charleston Receipts* cookbook."

(Yep, it's the second-most-followed book in the South, next to the Bible.)

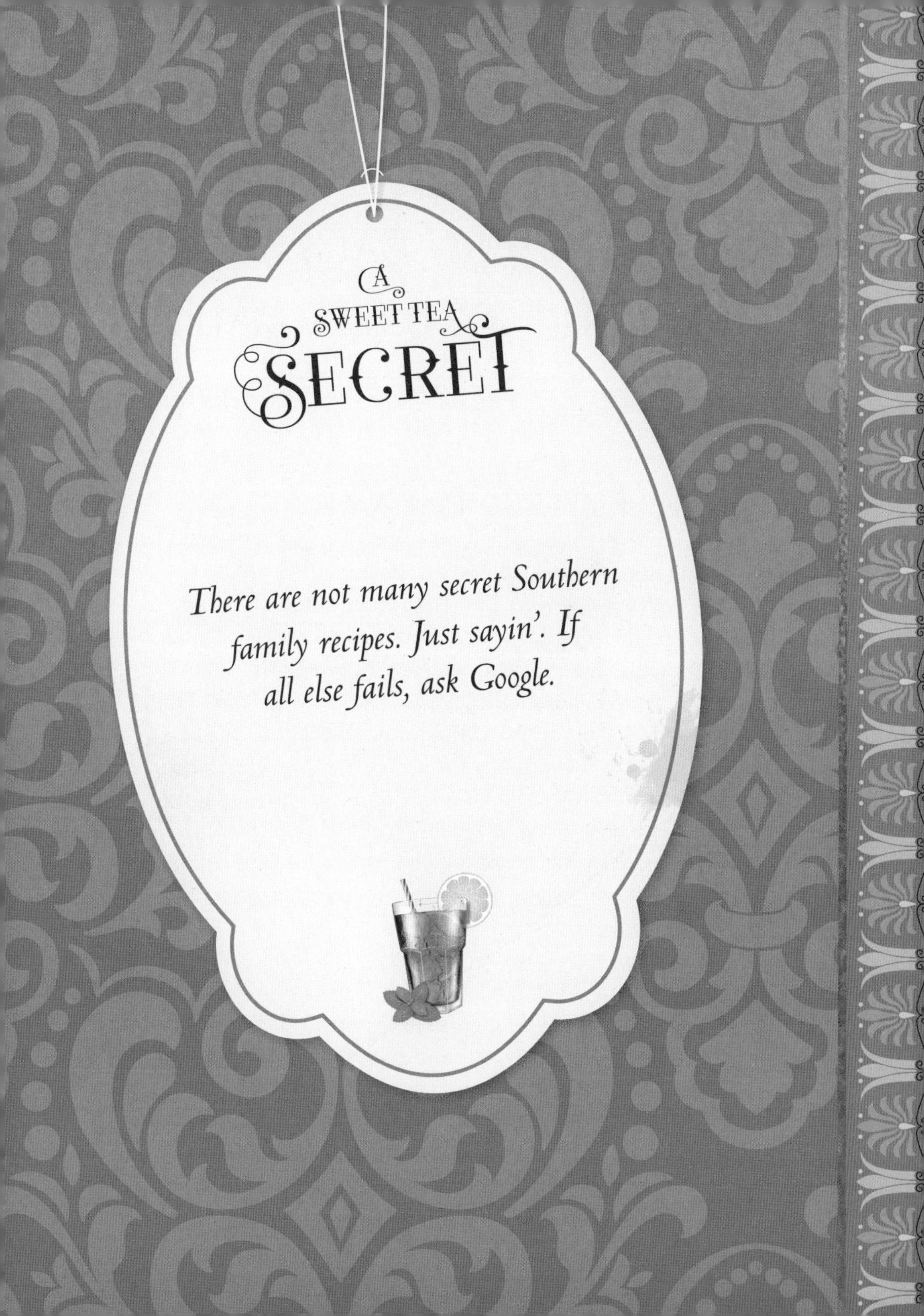
A SWEET TEA SECRET
There are not many secret Southern family recipes. Just sayin'. If all else fails, ask Google.

37

SOUTHERN GALS AND SACRED FOOTBALL GAMES

MORE RELIGION THAN RITUAL, college football in the South is both New York's Fashion Week and a Paula Deen food-and-fun feast. Matters not if it is 101 degrees out with 100 percent humidity, a Southern woman will dress to steal your date while toting a pot of Parmesan-jalapeño grits and a cooler filled with enough desserts to trigger type 2 diabetes. Her entourage—date, boyfriend, husband, whoever the lucky lad is—trails behind her, pulling a cart loaded with a generator, grill, fans, big-screen TV, tables, chairs, and enough decorations for a mobile home park. A rainbow of the team colors, logos, and mascots printed on tablecloths, tents, hanging lanterns, umbrellas, and even cupcakes mark the boundary lines of loyalties. I know what you're thinking: Folks up North tailgate too. But honey, it's not the same. Not even close.

For one, New England "tail-gators" talk funny and ask ridiculous stuff like "Where can I pock my cah?" when it's clear from the signs staked into the grass along the road leading to the stadium that you cannot park your car anywhere near our hallowed turf. Carpetbaggers traveling down from north of the Mason-Dixon Line are relegated to the shuttle lot. New Yorkers use words like *mudder* a lot. I'm not 100 percent sure what they mean by *mudder,* but their loud spraying of spittle suggests that my momma, God rest her soul, would have insisted that stadium security order such persons to wash their mouths out with soap before being allowed to sit in our visitor section.

For another, Yankee women don't dress properly on game day. They may wear a team jersey with the number of their favorite player. But that kind of half-hearted attempt isn't acceptable at a Southern football game. Southern women dress in their team's colors from head to toe—matching earrings, mascot necklaces, monogrammed shoes. Even their underwear is team-themed, for good luck. Their lipstick matches the team's color too. On the side of their cheek is a tattoo of the team's mascot—tiger, gamecock, gator, dawg, elephant, dragon . . . the list goes on.

Once Thomas and I traveled to Syracuse for a Clemson away game. Niagara Falls was frozen over; snow paths in the parking lot hinted at where cars might have once parked. When we arrived, the rows and rows of vehicles resembled moguls on ski slopes. God love 'em, a clot of Syracuse fans stood around a rusty gas grill, trying to cook a piece of meat that I can only imagine came from a recently excavated woolly mammoth discovered in a melting glacier.

The bare-chested Syracuse fans warming themselves beside the grill reminded me of our Southern female football fans who bare too much of their bodies at the first hint of spring. As older, seasoned Southern women, we feel duty bound to approach our own kind and ask, "Now what would your Momma think of you dressing like that? Honey, instead of showing cleavage, you should be smart and use *cleverage*."

Competition is fierce on game day, and if we can run up the score, we will. Ours is a blood sport where the goal is to out-host your fellow Southern sistah to the point where next time she'll think twice or three times before bringing a bucket of store-bought KFC to the game. If you haven't put the hours in Monday through Friday, don't even bother to show up on Saturday. Arrive early and stay late, but above all else, look good and eat well.

True to Southern hospitality, we expect to have guests stop by and sample our food. Often no one in the tailgating party knows these random strangers. They could be, as one person in the Bible put it, visitors from outside the conference. "Don't forget to show hospitality to strangers, for some who have done this have entertained angels without realizing it!"

(Hebrews 13:2, NLT). So in keeping with that biblical admonition, fans from other teams are invited to graze our football cuisine. For some this might be the only real home-cooked meal they get all year.

A few years back, legendary 1981 National Champ Clemson head coach Danny Ford parked his cattle truck near our space. That's right: Danny Ford arrived in a manure-scented, mud-covered utility farm vehicle. Since he was Danny Ford, he did not have to say something ridiculous like "Where can I pock my track?" Danny is a living legend to us Tigers fans, so he is welcome to "pock" that "track" in all its glory anywhere. We all knew Danny liked apple-crunch cake, so there was a lot of it at Clemson home games in hopes that he'd swing by and have a bite. Folks walking by would stop, stare, and whip out cell phones for a shot of Danny sampling a sistah's apple-crunch cake.

Danny loves to tell about the time when our good bud Keva Jackson's heart stopped, and he collapsed. "I was standing right by Keva when he went down," Danny says. "Practically got on top of him to do mouth-to-mouth. Thank the Lord, right then Keva's heart defibrillator kicked in. When he opened his eyes, the first thing he saw was me 'bout to kiss him on the lips. Quick as a linebacker blitz, Keva said, 'I've died and gone to hell!'"

But we all know that in reality if Keva had chosen when to go, it would have been in the presence of his orange idol in, ironically, Death Valley, Clemson University's stadium. Or to quote country singer Paul Craft, "Dropkick me, Jesus, through the goalposts of life."

In the South, football is religion, but it's not *the* religion. So if you come south for a game, plan to stand for the Pledge of Allegiance and the singing of the national anthem, and then bow your head for the game prayer.

Ready to score with another sip of Southern sweet tea from a tall glass? In the South, we'll tolerate most things, even store-bought KFC if that's the best you can do, but when it comes to God and patriotism, you'd best show respect.

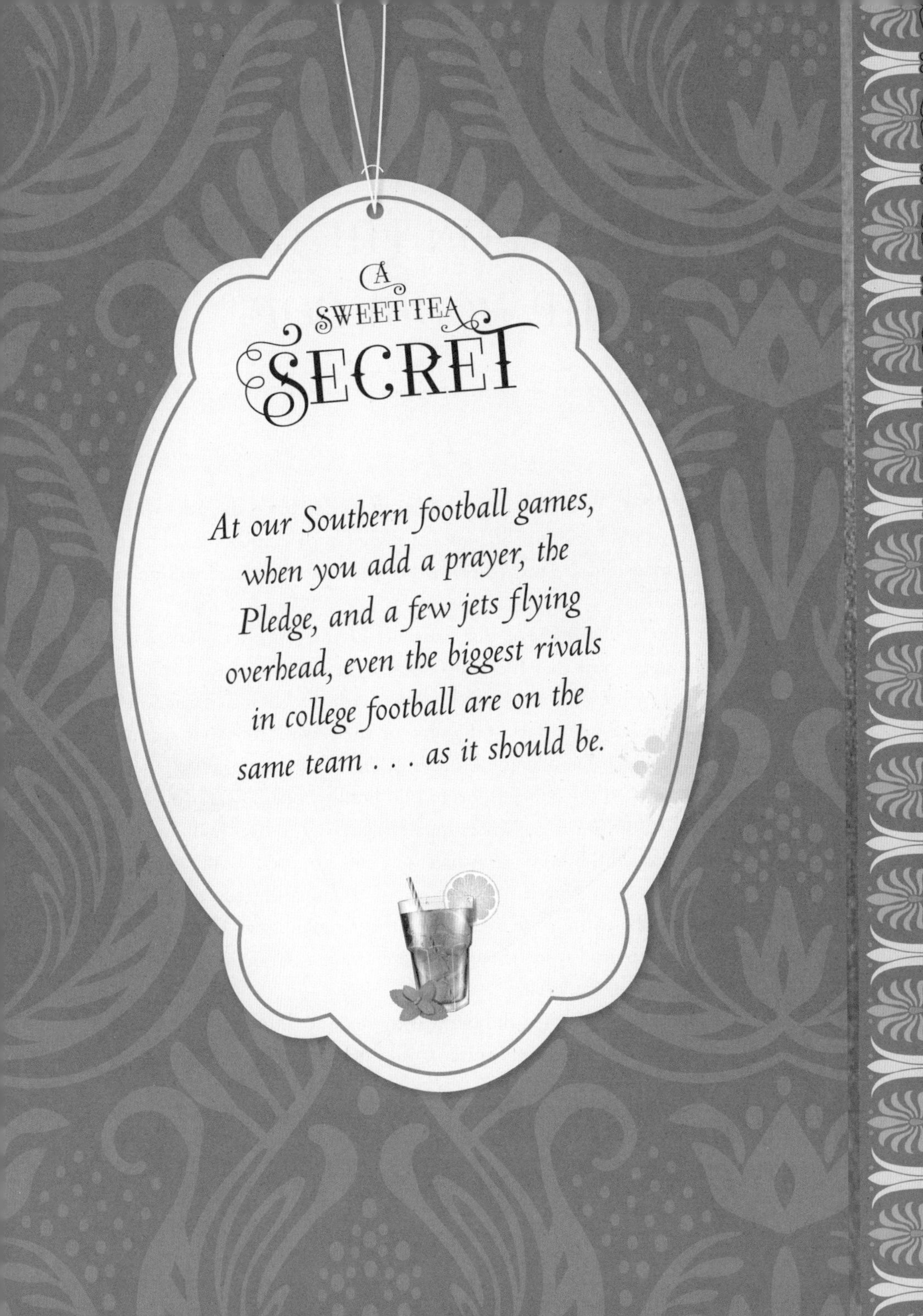
A
SWEET TEA
SECRET
At our Southern football games, when you add a prayer, the Pledge, and a few jets flying overhead, even the biggest rivals in college football are on the same team . . . as it should be.

38

SAILING ON THE GOOD SHIP *BOBBY BOP*

MOST WOMEN in the South love to travel in packs with their own kind and hit the high seas. My family's cruise introduced me to an alternative way to enjoy these excursions—one I will never forget.

On the first night of our cruise we hit a storm. Actually, we hit the karaoke show that ended up worse than a storm at sea. I angled towards a pack of middle-aged women with thick Southern accents who appeared to be having the time of their lives. Every few seconds one of the gals would squeal, "Bobby, dance with me next."

I searched the dance floor, but no Bobby bobbing could I see. Then I spied him in a corner, apparently trying to hide. Tall, tanned, with a beautiful head of gray hair. The gals pounced. Bobby and this pack of women danced, ate, imbibed, and sang at the top of their lungs for the entire time we endured the karaoke show. The climax of the storm arrived when the women even pulled Bobby onto the stage so all of them could sing "We Are Family."

When later I spied Bobby weaving his way through the crowded dance floor, I pulled him aside. "Couldn't help but notice that rowdy crowd you were with."

"Yes, I am responsible for these women. They love to go on cruises, and their husbands don't want to go, so they hire me to organize their trip, entertain them, and especially make sure they are safe and stay out of trouble. Their husbands are on a golfing trip. Makes for a happy marriage, I guess, but my feet aren't so happy right about now."

The next morning on my walk around the ship, I stumbled upon a corpse. Okay, not really, but sacked out in a lounge chair wearing a robe, slippers, towel on his head, and sunglasses, he looked dead to the world.

"Bobby?"

"I'm begging you, please don't tell them where I am. If you want to help at all, pray the good Lord'll come and take me before these women do."

Throughout the rest of the trip, Bobby was loaded down with bags of souvenirs, hats, shoes, and all things cruise worthy.

The last I saw of Bobby he was hiding behind a bunker of suitcases constructed to provide maximum protection and concealment. Above the handle of a paisley Ricardo Del Mar softside spinner, the tippy-top peak of ruffled gray hair poked up. I couldn't help but think that those husbands had been right smart to hire Bobby as their wives' escort and pack mule.

God bless the Bobbys of this world, but as time goes on, Southern women may find they covet those times when we sit with our hubbies and stare out across water without saying a word. Silence is golden. This is especially so for those of us easing into our golden years. Travel with a Bobby if you want, but when the one you promised to love until death is gone, you'll long for those routine, mundane moments more than any other.

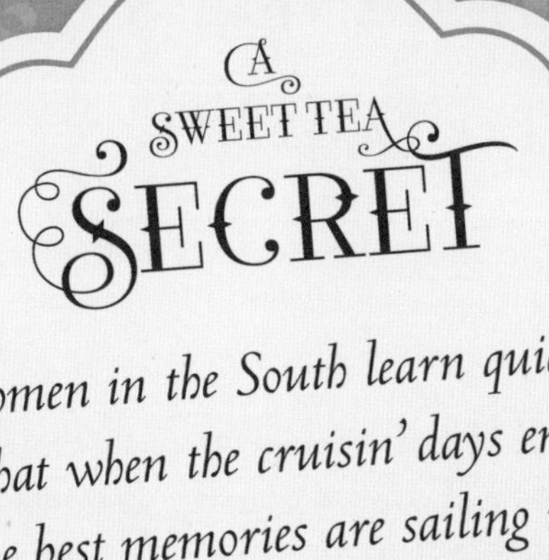

Women in the South learn quickly that when the cruisin' days end, the best memories are sailing into a Southern sunset on your own personal love boat, holding hands with the captain of your dreams. This year give thanks for the one you love and who loves you.

39

The Yankees Are Coming!

WHO ARE THESE strangers from another land? Although we take pride in our Southern traditions, we do embrace foreigners who honor our unspoken code: Love us and don't try to change us, and we, in turn, will do the same.

I knew these visitors were from New York, but they proudly added a prefix before stating their state—apparently it was more important to them than the I-95 corridor. And what is this all-important word? *Upstate.* Being from Upstate New York rather than New York City makes one's journey more acceptable to pass below the Mason-Dixon Line.

The only thing I knew was that once a year, right after Christmas, Bryan and Percilla VanFleet would hook up their Airstream camper and pull it all the way from Trumansburg, New York, to Jenkins Farm Road and park in our yard. Seeing their silver Airstream wind down our dirt road was like Christmas morning all over again. The VanFleets would stay for months on end, then continue their journey until they arrived at the Tangerine Cove somewhere in Florida.

Daddy became acquainted with the VanFleets' son, Bud, since Bud drove 18-wheelers filled with tomatoes from Johns Island, up North and back down South during the Lowcountry harvest. Daddy was fascinated with folks from all walks of life and made it perfectly clear that the VanFleets were not really Yankees—they were Dutch.

Bryan and Percilla VanFleet were a curious couple to a young child. First of all, Percilla is not a Southern name unless there is a hyphen or middle name like Percilla-Sue or Percilla-Anne.

Unlike my mother, who had her hair fixed religiously every Wednesday at 9 a.m. at Belks department store, Percilla used another technique. Her hairdo was done by our metal teakettle. Percilla would heat the water to the boiling point then hover her head over the steam to curl her hair.

Percilla also wore white ankle socks and Keds tennis shoes. My mother's shoes of choice were stilettos that were practically registered weapons. I don't believe I ever saw my mother wearing a pair of Keds, much less white socks. Until the day my mother passed away, she fondly referred to white ankle socks as *Percillas.*

My sister and I called our Yankee-Dutch Airstream Queen the Southern version of Percilla—Mrs. VanFleet. We watched her work crossword puzzles in *Reader's Digest* while my mother listened to her favorite singers on our LP record player. Percilla loved painting little pictures while Momma sat at our kitchen table painting her nails fire-engine red. Percilla played solitaire while my mother perfected a mean hand of poker. To say they were different is a massive understatement.

Bless Tootsie's heart; she had no idea what "dem peoples" were saying since she spoke fluent Gullah and they spoke Dutch-Yankee. I became the translator on many occasions. Tootsie never could understand why the VanFleets thought Cream of Wheat was grits.

Daddy came up with a description of Percilla's accent. He said that Yankees (but remember, they were more Dutch than Yankee) sound just like a meowing overheated cat.

And when Bryan and Percilla had a spat—and who wouldn't, after being stuck in a silver-shaped bullet for months—her name became one of Daddy's favorite adjectives. "Eleanor," Daddy would exclaim, "don't go Percilla on me . . ." I never knew what Daddy meant by saying that, but one

thing I did know was that Eleanor nixed the Keds and never would have teakettle hair.

The summer of '67, Daddy made some money from his tomato crop; my sister, brother, parents, and I stuffed ourselves into Daddy's brand-new two-toned Pontiac with the white hard top and traveled nonstop to Trumansburg, New York, to visit our Yankee/Dutch friends. Did you catch the word *nonstop*? It was one of the most miserable weeks of my life.

The famed tourist attraction Taughannock Falls was an epic failure since there was no water at the waterfall. Watkins Glen was nothing more than a pile of rocks, and the only exciting event was when Momma got a new set of dishes from the Corning Museum of Glass. The highlight of the trip should have been Niagara Falls, but my sister ate too much chocolate and threw up in Daddy's new car, which started a family throw-up chain reaction. Interstate South was calling my name.

So the years passed and the VanFleets were no longer able to haul their Airstream down the I-95 corridor to Johns Island. One day, we received the sad news that Percilla had passed away. Sweet Mr. VanFleet kept up with my family and wrote us on a regular basis. His letters were mostly about his small farm and the weather; sadly, his correspondence became less frequent and his handwriting barely legible. Until one day when I was a contestant in the Miss America Pageant and he wrote me the sweetest note telling me how proud he was and how dear his memories were of visits to our little country home down that long dirt road.

How fortunate I am to have known Bryan and Percilla VanFleet.

Learning how to love strangers from another land who talk funny, don't eat grits, wear white ankle socks, and curl their hair with steam from an old teakettle makes a very precious memory.

PART VII

Southern Royalty

40

There She Is

THE ROOM IS suddenly quiet. Eyes toggle. Everyone's gaze drifts toward the woman standing with her hair perfectly groomed, swept to the side. Wearing power shoes with a pop of color, she's perfected her makeup to complement her natural features. Without overpowering her God-given good looks, her outfit speaks for itself: She's radiant! She commands the room with perfect posture as her eyes sweep from left to right. Who is this stunning creature? That's the question on everyone's mind.

Then a whisper explains it all. "You know, she is a former 'Catfish Feastival Queen.'" Instantly those in the room understand they are in the company of something like royalty.

Those of us in the Southern beauty pageant sorority teach our offspring how to become a head-turner, make a statement, and be a powerhouse, an achiever of their best selves. Many times, this evolution has humble beginnings.

For some, the beauty-pageant league is the ultimate in women's sport. Although the athleticism is seldom seen, it's there. You'll find these athletes in the gym, in the pool, on stationary bikes, and on all manner of balls and mats. To work that body into shape requires effort and determination. Ours is not a cheap sport. The cost of equipment precludes many from competition. Oh sure, early-on commoners can run with the society gals, but without sponsors, eventually they're priced out by the cost of shoes, dresses, hair coloring, and so much more.

As in all sports, the game ends; then the stars fade and the chins fall or sag as do many of those other natural features you ride to great heights. Left with tarnished crowns and fading photographs, Miss Whatever retreats to her vanity and with a sigh (and sometimes tears) thinks back to what she once was.

Some just can't let it go and have to have their face on at all times. One former state queen was allegedly paid an early, unexpected visit by a plumber, and she did not have her face on. As the story goes, she grabbed a paper bag, cut eyeholes, made lashes, and wore the bag over her head to answer the door. Several queens to this day express their admiration and respect for her ingenuity.

I asked my friend Dixie to go with me to the Miss South Carolina forum for beauty queen wannabes. What I failed to tell her was that the age range of the queen lineup extended from a three-month-old baby to over twenty-five years old. In pageant world, if you have the entry fee, there is a special trophy just for you.

As we rounded the corner at the Spartanburg Hilton, we saw a toddler with a pacifier in her mouth, carrying a teddy bear. A crown complemented her blonde curls, and draped across her torso was a sash with glittered letters spelling "Little Miss Pull-It." To this day, Dixie will randomly comment, "I wonder whatever happened to that poor child wearing the crown with the pacifier. Could that have been Honey Boo Boo?"

Perhaps. Or maybe "Little Miss Pull-It" went on to become Miss CEO.

Southerners are royally entertained by these crazy titles and pageants, but many Southern queens achieve amazing things after they become involved in the world of Southern pageantry. Something magical happens when a young woman challenges herself to achieve excellence. That's the other thing about the beauty pageant league: It instills confidence.

Scholarship interviews, dinners with prospective employers, and first dates take courage and poise. If you lack confidence in yourself, you may as well not even bother.

I have no idea what happened to "Little Miss Pull-It," but I bet she made something of herself. Maybe she pulled herself up into something beautiful and made herself into a confident woman. And I bet her family is glad she did. It's a beautiful thing when we decide to pull, push, or propel ourselves into a challenge. We should all be pulling for the Little Miss Pull-Its of the world . . . crown or no crown.

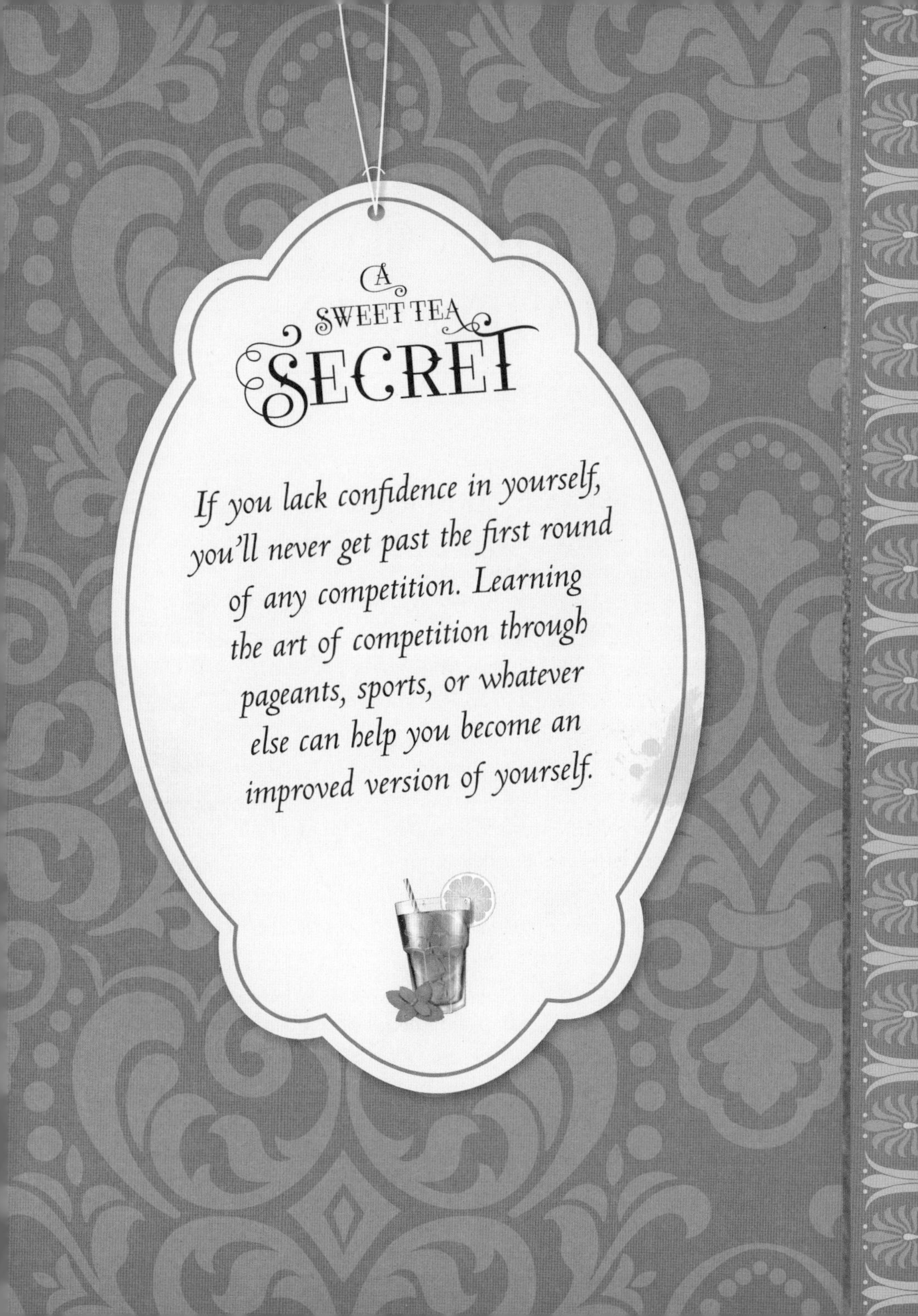
A SWEET TEA SECRET
If you lack confidence in yourself, you'll never get past the first round of any competition. Learning the art of competition through pageants, sports, or whatever else can help you become an improved version of yourself.

41
THE UGLY BEAUTY QUEEN

MY PAGEANT CAREER began in the first grade. No, I was not a child beauty contestant. I was a fired-up-mad Little Miss Merry Christmas shoulda-been.

"Y'all look cute tomorrow," said my first-grade teacher. "The high school girls are coming to our class to select who will compete for the coveted title of Little Miss Merry Christmas." Well, that title had my name all over it . . . or so I thought.

Only problem the day of judging was my wardrobe. Being a tomboy, I wore corduroy pants, a flannel shirt, and penny loafers. I had brushed my hair and shined the coins in my shoes. I was looking fine for a girl with oversized lips and a gap in her smile where my two front teeth had been. But that didn't stop me from marching myself to the front of the classroom and smiling big as a mule. Snickers and lots of whispering rippled across the room when I took my place next to our class diva.

Debra Sue was my rival, and her momma had dressed her in a stick-out (crinoline) dress, poodle socks, and her Easter shoes. Because her momma had a local connection with the Avon lady, who also worked in the bookmobile, bright red lipstick coated Debra Sue's normal-sized lips. Her hair was a mass of ringlets and bows, glued in place by Extra Super Hold Aqua Net. In other words, "Her hair was jacked up to Jesus." She knew it, she flaunted it, and

I silently wished I could get my hair to look so good—or get back my teeth—for the big event.

It wasn't like we'd had a lot of notice or training, so most of us stood on stage, sheepishly shifting from one foot to the other, while the high school girls eyed us with serious looks. These girls were beauty goddesses, for goodness' sake, and would anoint someone as first-grade pretty. Of course, the judges picked Debra Sue Aqua Net Hair to be our representative.

I attended that first-grade pageant, where I sat on a broken chair and watched Debra Sue and the other contestants in beehive hairdos tromp across that old high school stage. I was so envious, God could have sent me to hell for craving the honor of Little Miss Merry Christmas contestant, and I wouldn't have cared.

As it turned out, God was watching and listening to my jealous heart. That evening, as I was sitting in a broken chair, he spoke to me in the way only the God of Broken Dreams can speak. I knew right there and then, God had planted a seed in my heart. He loved me enough to begin a process that warmed my heart with a fire and conviction that fueled my determination to succeed.

So when anger turns into determination, good things can happen. I was determined to walk on that iconic Miss America stage in Atlantic City, New Jersey. I had a plan.

I studied past winners, read a book titled *How to Smile,* had my oversized thighs sprayed with heaven-knows-what to reduce the size of my legs. I also hired a voice and showmanship coach; worked with a funeral home director at his funeral home in Sumter, South Carolina (to look more alive, not dead); and learned how to beauty-queen-walk and beauty-queen-talk.

Seventeen years and five months later, I stood on the stage of the Miss America Pageant.

When things don't work out, don't be bitter. Be determined to be better. God can work better in your life if you ditch the bitterness. Like my momma said, "You can get more out of life with honey than you can with vinegar." That's the sweetest of sweet tea advice, minus the lemon.

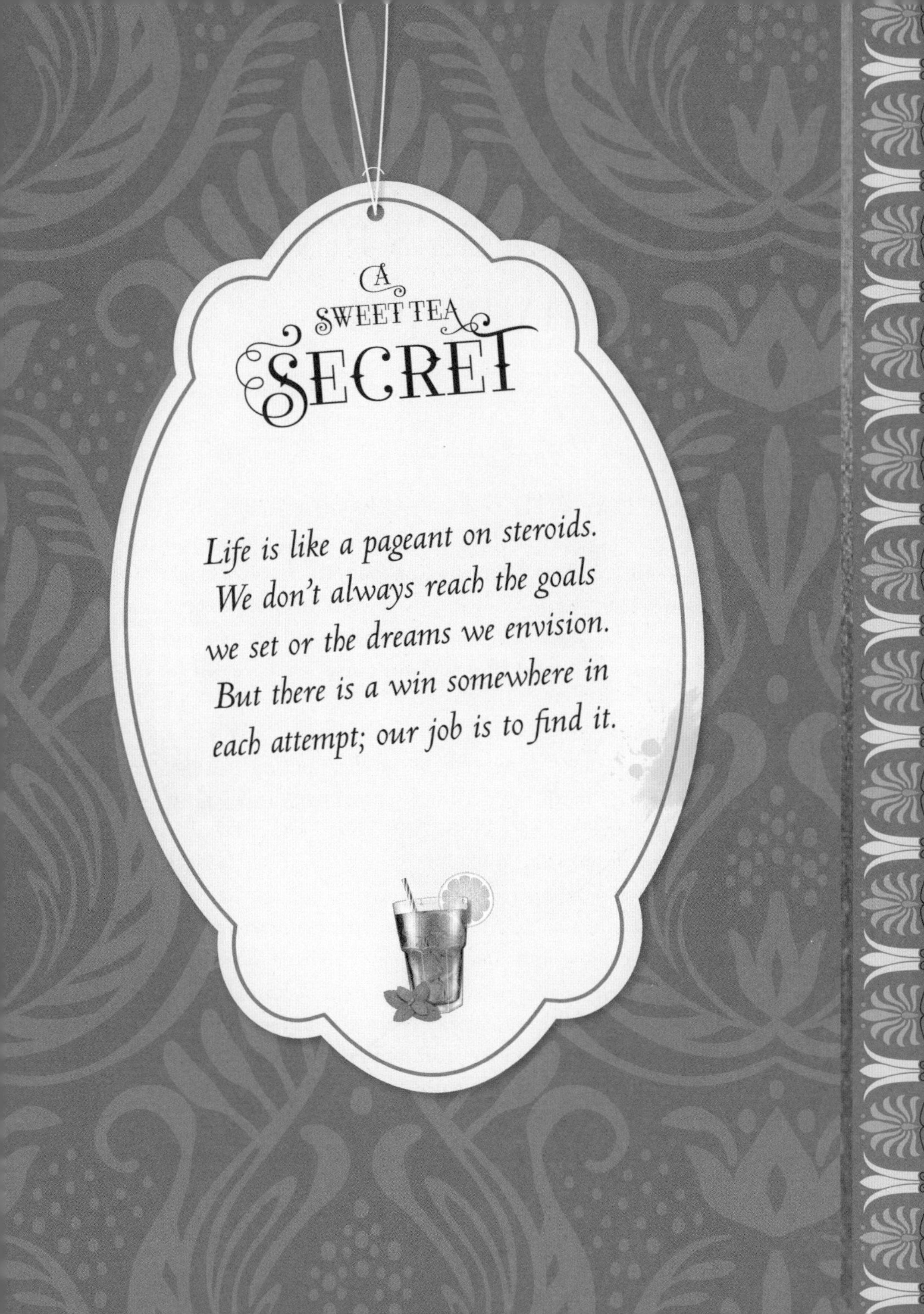
A SWEET TEA SECRET
Life is like a pageant on steroids. We don't always reach the goals we set or the dreams we envision. But there is a win somewhere in each attempt; our job is to find it.

42 MOMMA'S PINK HAIR PICK

ONE DAY WHEN I was rummaging around the bottom of my purse, I felt an unexpected twinge of pain from some metal prongs—my mother's infamous pink hair pick. I always figured that thing would be the death of her. Even when her heart was beating in a deadly, life-threatening rhythm, I had to find the pink pick and place it in the inner pocket of her purse before she left for the hospital.

Momma never missed her hair appointment, and the pink hair pick was a constant accessory in my mother's purse.

When my mother's internist suspected that she had sleep apnea, he instructed her to wear "that Thing" on her face. Well, the apparatus was short lived. It messed up her hair. The doctor reluctantly allowed her to sleep with oxygen.

I tried to explain to Momma that since her heart could use all the help it could get, the machine might give her a longer life. She needed to go for a sleep study; without the CPAP machine, she might die in her sleep. She responded, "That's just fine. Johnny Stuhr [Stuhr Funeral Home] will think my hair looks nice."

Daddy once said that he knew his funeral would be planned around Momma's hair appointment. I'm taking the Fifth Amendment on that issue.

During one hospital stay, Momma's hemoglobin dropped

to 5.8. She was under the care of Dr. Theodore Gourdin, a wonderful gastroenterologist. When he came to see her, he said, "You're the best looking 5.8 hemoglobin I've seen in a long time."

Of course, my mother took that as a compliment. She smiled, puffed her hair with her hand, and said, "Oh, thank you so much!"

Dr. Gourdin laughed, puffed his own hair with his hand, and said, "You're welcome."

After that, every time I saw him in the halls of Roper Hospital, he always commented on my mother's reaction, then puffed his hair. Our little joke. He loved my mother—said she was the consummate Southern lady. After she passed away, he wrote me a lovely note that I treasure to this day.

The hair pick symbolized Momma's beauty inside and out. She always dressed well, stylish from her head to her toes.

My mother loved people, she had a forgiving heart, and she loved to laugh. Those are timeless beauty products we would all be wise to pick.

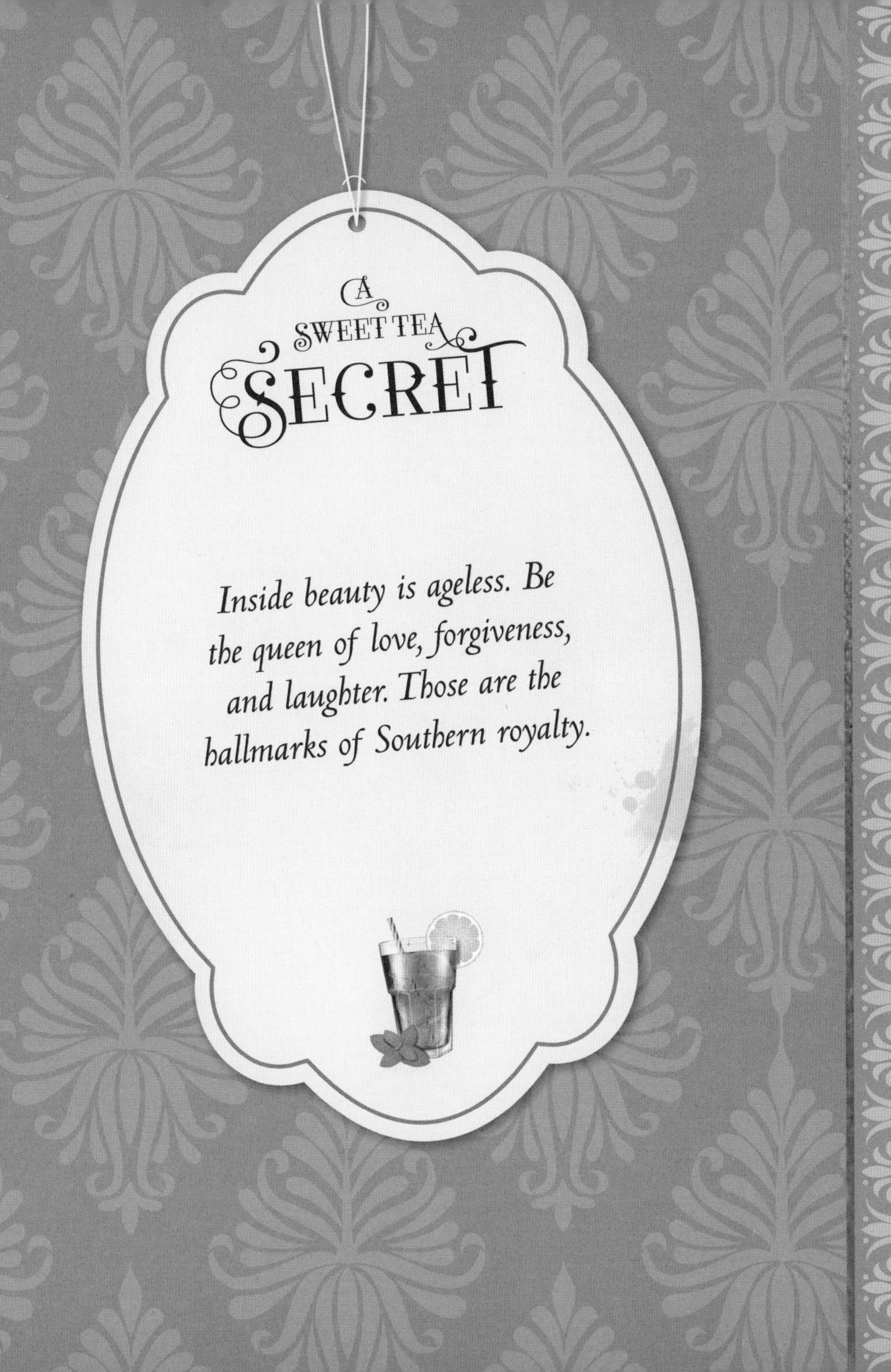
A
SWEET TEA
SECRET
Inside beauty is ageless. Be
the queen of love, forgiveness,
and laughter. Those are the
hallmarks of Southern royalty.

PART VIII

Sassy, Seasoned Southern Women

43

Timeless Beauty— Southern Style

OVER A PERIOD of two months, Momma had open-heart surgery, then a trip to ICU, on to the third floor at Roper Hospital, back to ICU once again, and finally rehab. My sister, Carol, and I learned lots of interesting things about Momma when she was parked in ICU. Her sense of humor was transformed into a very vivid imagination. Every morning when we were allowed into ICU, she would point her suction tube at various doctors and nurses and describe in great detail her accounts of their late-night rendezvous. The best story was the one about the nurse who flew off with Dr. McSteamy in a helicopter that ended up landing by Momma's bed. Her stories were so entertaining that the guilty parties stood around her bed and asked her to tell them over and over.

We knew Eleanor was ready to go back to the third floor when she asked if her hairdresser could come to ICU. She actually made history at Roper Hospital. My mother was the only woman at the time to have her hair done in ICU, minus the hair spray. (Oxygen and hair spray don't play well together.)

When we finally returned home, it was tough seeing my fun-loving, beautiful, super-seasoned Southern mother become thin and frail and struggle to negotiate her way up the stairs with a walker. I fought tears as I tried to steady her while she bumped along. After step number three, the rubber tip on her walker got stuck between two boards. At first Momma was patient, but that didn't last long. She flung her walker in the air. It landed a good eight feet away, barely missing the kitchen table. Walkerless, she shuffled down that hall like a woman on a mission. The healing process had begun.

Momma got better. In doing so, she taught me to add humor to challenging moments. One way I remember Momma's legacy is to celebrate her sweet tea moments. I relax on my front porch with a tall glass of said beverage, where I reflect on her influence and my own success. It helps keep me both humble and encouraged.

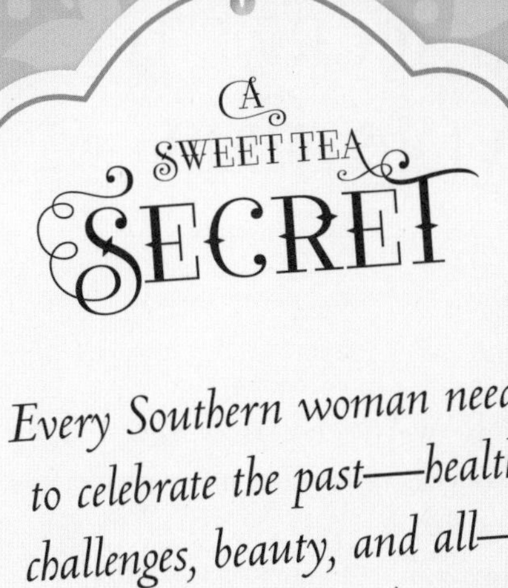

A Sweet Tea Secret

Every Southern woman needs to celebrate the past—health challenges, beauty, and all—and remember that it's not our looks people remember, but the way we looked at, touched, helped, and encouraged others.

44
The Secret to Living Well

My mother was a star. Every time I took her with me to a speaking engagement, folks fell in love with her quick wit and unfiltered comments.

I was booked to speak to an agricultural group at the Homestead in West Virginia. I had always wanted to speak at this iconic convention property, and I knew my mother would enjoy seeing the beautiful Allegheny Mountains. The meeting planner was more than gracious, agreeing for my mother to join me on this speaking engagement.

On the last night of the convention, Momma and I were invited to have dinner with the entire board and other special guests. We all sat around a long banquet table; my mother and I sat near the middle next to the CEO. The meal was delicious, and the assortment of bite-size treats served afterward was amazing. As we all passed the desserts to one another, the CEO began conversing with my mother. I knew Momma did not know who anyone was and she couldn't have cared less. Momma was always herself.

"Mrs. Jenkins, how are things on Johns Island? Do you stay busy?" asked the CEO.

"Yes," commented my mother as she helped herself to another dessert. "I had two doctors' appointments last week. I visited my eye doctor and my gynecologist."

Oh, brother, I thought. *I hope this conversation stops here.*

As my mother finished her last bite of dessert, the CEO asked (referring to the pastry), "Now which one did you enjoy the most?"

"The gynecologist," she replied.

After a seemingly eternal pause, the entire table erupted in uncontrollable laughter. The meeting planner told me that my mother's comment was the highlight of the convention.

We have many iconic "Eleanor" moments.

After Momma's open-heart surgery, her internist referred her to a lung specialist, whom Momma referred to as Dr. Cootie (he had zero personality). He recommended that she be tested at a sleep lab for sleep apnea. Momma did not want to spend the night in a sleep lab and made the decision to stop going to Dr. Cootie. But when her breathing became worse, she reluctantly returned to his care; she knew this time she would have the dreaded sleep study. The test was finally scheduled for a Thursday night. However, Thursday was Momma's hairdo day with Rhea. Neither Hurricane Hugo, freak snowstorms, nor sickness kept her from sitting in Rhea's chair every week at 9:00 a.m.

It surprised me when Momma agreed to go to the sleep center only a few hours after getting her hair done. The staff couldn't have been any nicer. Everything was okay until they stuck a sticky electrode thing in Momma's hair. I cannot repeat what she said, but I knew it was time for me to leave.

When I arrived to retrieve Momma the next morning, I heard, "What do you mean I have sleep apnea? I didn't even sleep!"

I have to admit she was a trouper. She tried to adjust to "the machine"; she did give it a go. But then she made an executive decision that she could not tolerate the apparatus.

During one of Momma's many visits to Roper Hospital, her favorite physician, whom she referred to as Dr. Boyfriend, sat at her bedside and asked, "Mrs. Jenkins, are you using the machine?"

Just as serious as one can answer, Momma replied, "I cannot tolerate that CPAP smear up my nostrils."

The sophisticated and professional doctor laughed so hard that he almost rolled off the bed. I reminded Momma that the machine was not called a CPAP smear but a CPAP machine and that doctor was her cardiologist, not her gynecologist.

God bless my mother for always making so many people not only laugh but love her too.

The older I get, the more I realize the value of developing a great sense of humor.

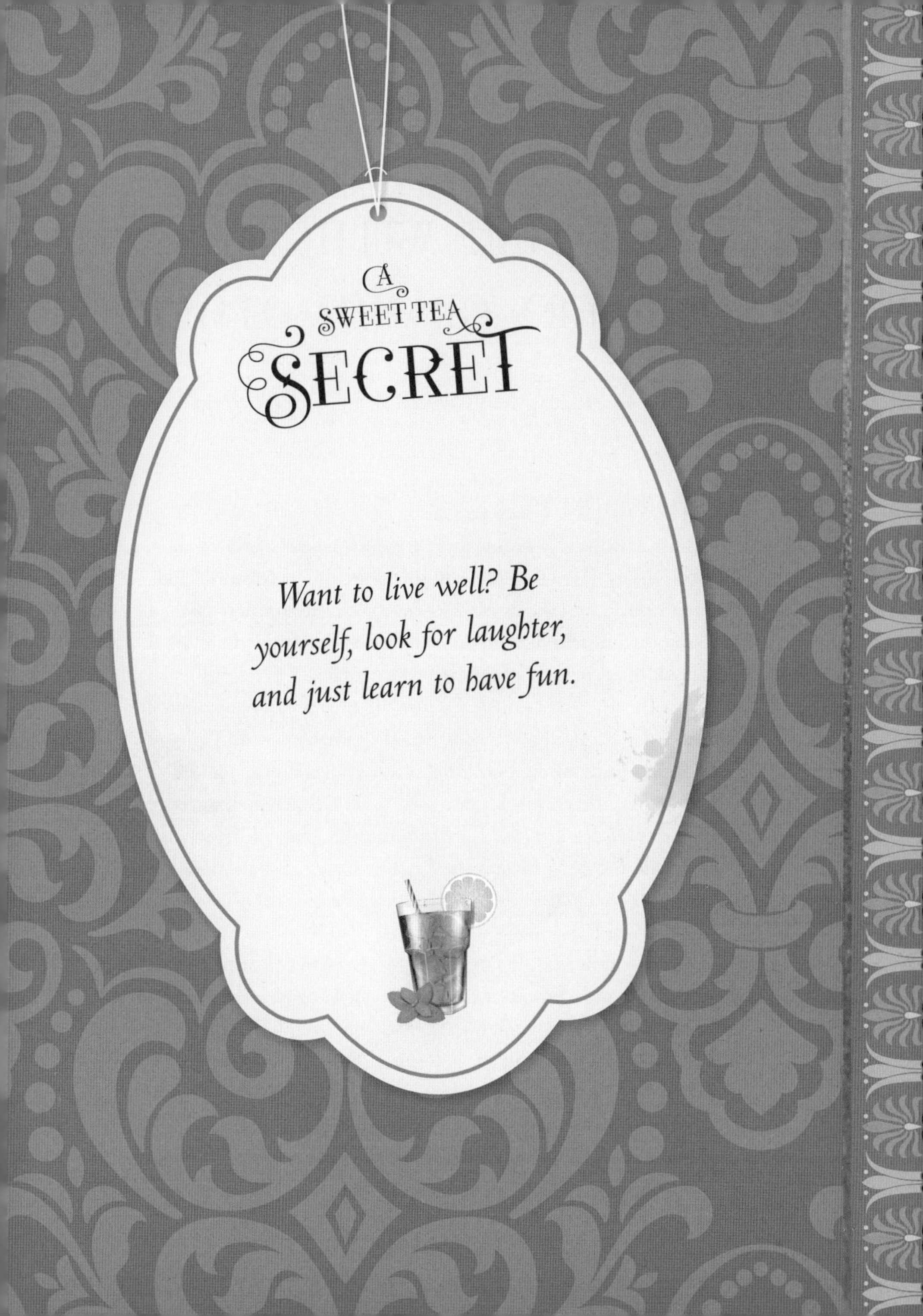
A
SWEET TEA
SECRET
Want to live well? Be
yourself, look for laughter,
and just learn to have fun.

45 Tee Time with the Southern Grandmother

THE WORD IS *tee,* not *tea.*

Our Southern grandmothers are a gift to us Southern churin'. They spoil us, hug us, feed us all the sweet things Momma and Daddy won't, and take us places where even the simplest task, like walking on a beach, becomes an adventure. And they do all of it with little risk of us getting popped on the bottom.

For those of us in the Carolinas, there is only one beach—it's south of Charlotte, Fayetteville, and Wilmington—and "going to The Beach" means you're heading toward Myrtle Beach and Ocean Drive. We Southern gals know a visit to The Beach is not complete until we enter the sacred shopping mecca known as The Shops at Pawleys Island, or more specifically, The Original Hammock Shop. It tugs at the tens, twenties, and credit cards of a Southern woman's wallet like a full moon on a flood tide.

Grandmother Becky is my idea of the perfect Southern grandma: an excellent cook, proud of her grandbabies, constantly worrying that her churin' have enough food, and able to find a bargain that others miss in a high-end shop. Some years back, she treated her two mischievous grandsons (one of them is now my son-in-law) with a visit to the Pawleys Island shops. She strapped them in the back seat and made her way to her first stop, the hammock shop.

As Grandma Becky walked through the shop, she noticed a golf

tee on the floor and stopped to pick it up. Only a few moments later, she spied another golf tee on the floor. Thinking a golfer in the shop had a hole-in-one (could not resist) of his pockets, she picked up that one too.

In typical grandmother style, she went about the store as if she were a golf pro's caddie walking the Masters course at Augusta. But on Grandma Becky's tour of the front nine (the easiest aisle), she gathered a foursome, then eightsome of perfectly good tees. She approached the main checkout counter and in her sweet Southern drawl said, "Hawn-ey, I found these gawf tees strewn all over the aisles, and I picked 'em up so no one in bare feet steps on 'em."

A smile spread across the clerk's face as she looked up at Grandma Becky, trying not to laugh. "Thanks, but they're not ours, ma'am. Those golf tees are coming from your hair."

Turns out that on the ride to The Shops at Pawleys Island, the two grandsons in the back seat used Grandma Becky's hair as a target while they threw "darts."

Some grandmothers would scold boys for such mischief, maybe even pop their little bottoms, but Grandma Becky simply smiled and with a slight head tilt said, "Hmmm . . . now I know why you boys were so quiet sitting back there."

But Grandma Becky doesn't forget. (Well, she forgets some things but not important stuff.) Years later at her grandson's wedding rehearsal dinner, she could have told the whole tee story while standing before the groom's cake, which was smeared with icing the color of turf green and covered with—you guessed it—golf tees. That would have been a clever payback, but that one mischievous-grandson story represents one hundred more. Grandma Becky was content to sit at her grandson's rehearsal dinner with a smile on her face and a multitude of memories tucked into her loving heart.

Grandma Becky is special, but she isn't unique. There are grandmas like Becky throughout the South and probably up in the North, too. If you have a special grandma story, email MyGrandma@janeherlong.com. If it's Grandma-Becky worthy, I'll share the story.

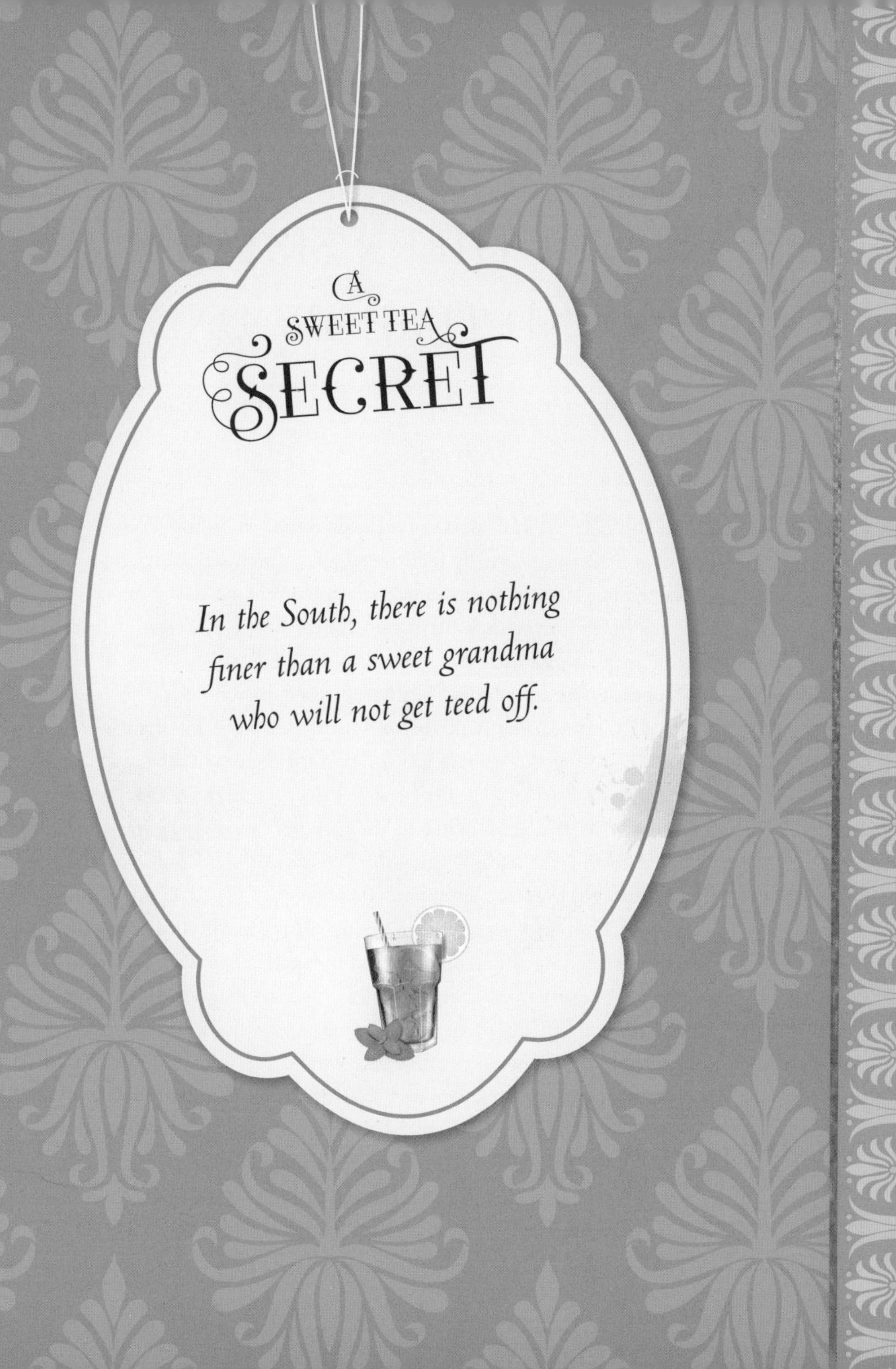
A SWEET TEA SECRET
In the South, there is nothing finer than a sweet grandma who will not get teed off.

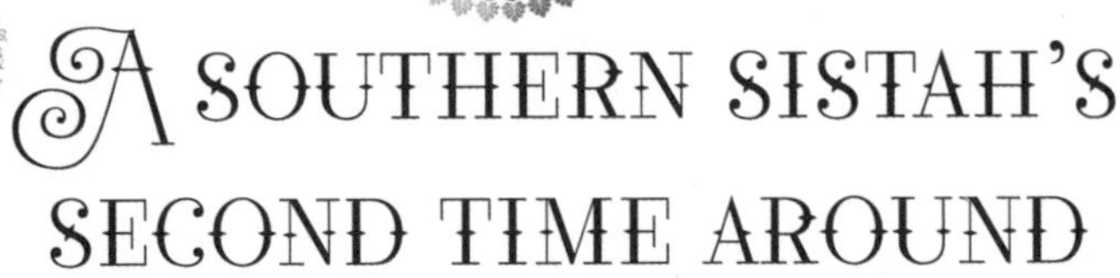

46 A Southern Sistah's Second Time Around

ONE OF MY dearest friends called me around the end of February 2020 and casually mentioned that a high school friend contacted her via text and told her he was coming to visit. She had not seen him in more than fifty years. Since she was widowed, I found this to be quite interesting.

After several visits, this Southern gentleman, who was also widowed, became a frequent visitor. During COVID-19, the only sickness affecting this couple was longing for the next visit-itus.

In August that year, at her home church, my friend walked into the arms of a wonderful man and changed her last name. I was honored to sing the song "Surely the Presence of the Lord Is in This Place." And his presence surely was there.

I told Thomas it seems when young people marry and promise "to love and to cherish in sickness and in health, for richer or poorer . . ." I don't think many couples grasp the magnitude of these vows until trouble hits them in the face or pocketbook. I know that only later did I fully understand those words.

At the altar, the beautiful exchange of smiles from two lovely people said it all. They understand the pain of loss, loneliness, and a sense of longing. They both are strong Christians and live their faith. They understand their vows completely. Both loved and cherished their first spouses and witnessed them pass away from the cruelty of cancer, each has had some health scares, and they understand financial ups and downs.

I wish there was some sort of magic wand for all couples to be able to see into their future. I hope and pray they can experience this same look in their eyes toward each other that I observed when my friend spoke her vows. Actually, I don't think I listened as much as I watched this beautiful union; during their ceremony, words seemed almost unnecessary.

By the way, did I mention these two lovebirds are nearing eighty years of age?

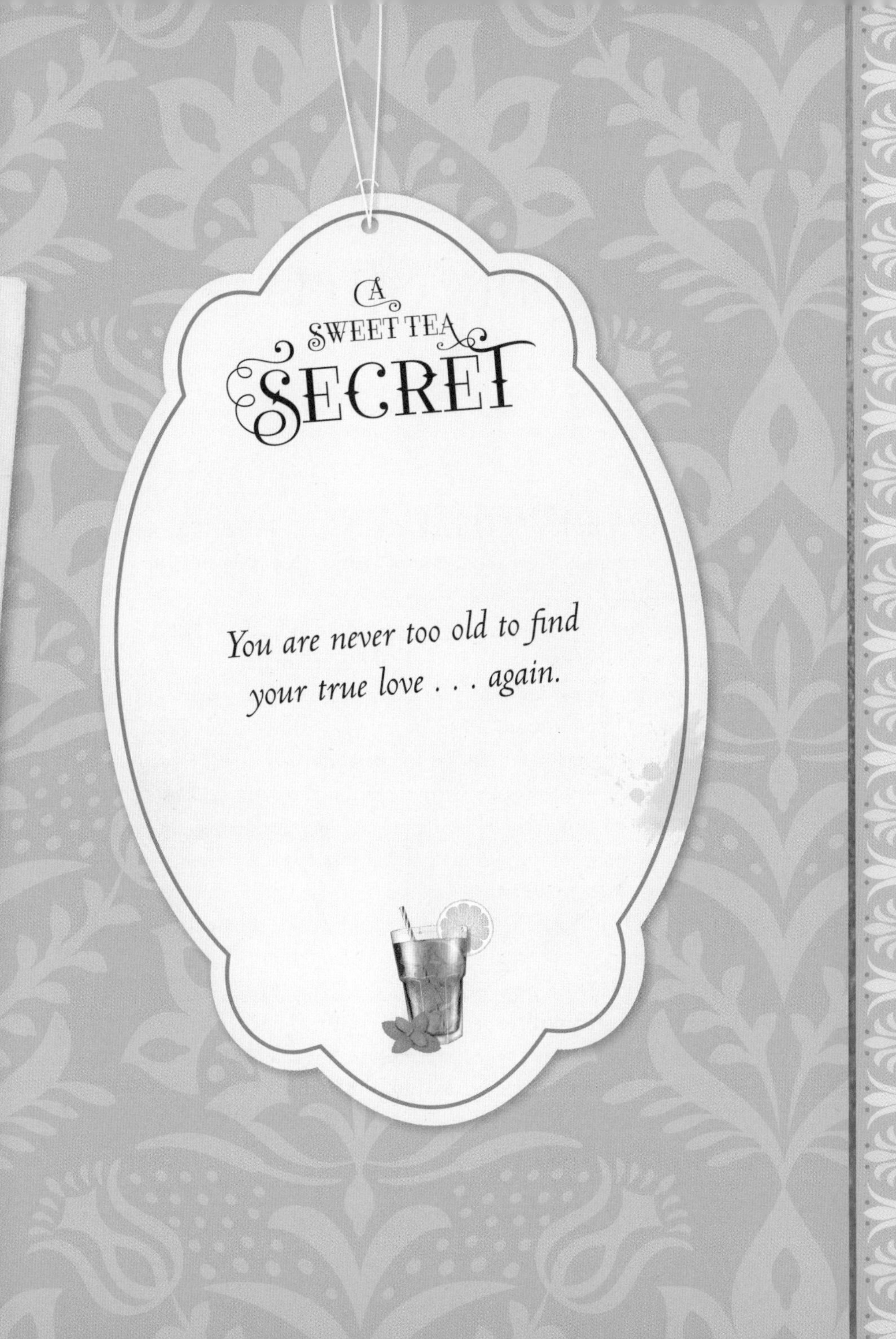
A
SWEET TEA
SECRET
You are never too old to find
your true love . . . again.

47

Cuddin' Titta

MY CUDDIN' TITTA LaRoach was a seasoned, gutsy Southern treasure. She had a sense of humor that is legendary on Johns Island.

As a child, I was fortunate enough to be in Cuddin' Titta's Sunday school class. Her wide smile and animated face made simple Bible stories almost jump off the pages of our Sunday school book. I particularly loved it when she made up a pet name for me: Janie Bird.

Many of our forefathers (or forepersons) who were reared during the Great Depression were the original recyclers; Cuddin' Titta was the poster child on how to repurpose and reuse.

Every morning she would cook her family a full, homegrown breakfast. One particular day Cuddin' Titta had no fresh eggs, so she went to her backyard chicken house. Loud clucks, squawks, and much commotion rang out from inside the chicken house. Cuddin' Titta saw the problem—a large, lumpy chicken snake. The hungry creature had helped itself to three eggs. Cuddin' Titta, the ultimate recycler, took off her shoes, held the snake upside down, and with her toes carefully negotiated the uncracked eggs in the opposite direction. The hungry snake slithered off, but Cuddin' Titta was able to cook her family a hearty breakfast.

I guess you can say that Cuddin' Titta was an expert on how to work things out, even retrieving eggs from a lumpy, hungry snake.

Cuddin' Titta's quick wit came in handy over and over again. Along with being an excellent homemaker, Cuddin' Titta was an amazing educator. After teaching for forty-two years, Cuddin' Titta's last day of school should have been filled with loving words and well-wishes for retirement. But that day Cuddin' Titta, with her wide eyes and entertaining sense of humor, taught her colleagues a great lesson. An irate parent burst into the classroom, upset over Cuddin' Titta giving her child an F on his report card. "I'm so angry with you, I have a good mind to knock your teeth down your throat!"

Cuddin' Titta kept her cool and said, "I'll save you the trouble." She took out her false teeth and handed them to the angry woman.

When all else fails, a good laugh is a powerful weapon.

Cuddin' Titta's son told me another story that spread across Johns Island about as quickly as kudzu. One summer afternoon, Cuddin' Titta took him casting for shrimp in a nearby creek. A unique technique to casting involves holding the net in your mouth while slinging the weighted mesh net into the creek. As Cuddin' Titta was in the middle of casting, her false teeth somehow followed. In a nanosecond, her teeth seemed to hang in midair, but not for long. With amazing reflexes, she threw the net, retrieved her teeth, and caught some shrimp.

Cuddin' Titta left Johns Island years ago. Now I imagine she is probably casting a golden net in a heavenly creek filled with shrimp with an *eggs*traordinary side dish. What impresses me is understanding the influence we have in our own creeks: the fact that what we harvest depends on how we cast. I am thankful to have filled my net with funny and poignant lessons taught by gutsy, seasoned Southern women.

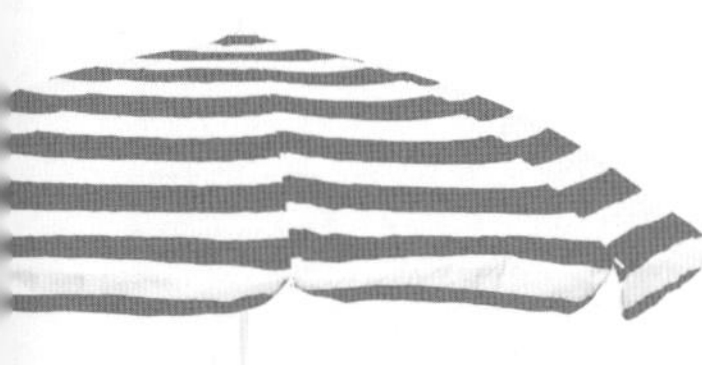

A
SWEET TEA
SECRET
Many relationships or circumstances in life cannot be fixed. The healthiest folks I know use humor or a relaxed attitude to handle those issues.

48

Lib Steadman's Legacy

IN OUR SMALL TOWN of Johnston lived a giant of a woman: Lib Steadman. She always had a smile on her face and prayer in her heart. When I heard of Mrs. Steadman's passing, I knew I had to share her unforgettable story.

Just to set the stage, Southern women are passionate about looking their best when leaving home. I always joked with my mother that her hair had not moved since 1962—the year Aqua Net was invented. Women in the South never forget the day they made the crucial mistake of not looking fabulous. And, of course, that's when they came face-to-face with old boyfriends, snobby Southern belles, the preacher, the hottie bug man, the postmaster, the town gossip. Being unprepared is an egregious act that goes against the unspoken code of a cultured Southern lady.

Lib never had to confess to that omission. She always looked beautiful. But being covered in prayer was more important to her than having makeup on her face. Lib believed that the Lord takes care of every detail; therefore, her top priority was to pray about everything, even down to parking her car.

Now to some this view may seem as over-the-top as leaving the house without earrings; how could you bother God with such minor details? After all, he is terribly busy.

Lib believed otherwise, so she asked the Lord to please watch over her and to provide the best parking space. And I can testify to the fact that those who ventured out with Lib were amazed that her parking space prayers were consistently answered.

My mother was curious about Lib's "parking prayer," so once when we were out shopping and circling the parking lot at Dillard's, she suddenly pointed to a parking spot and exclaimed, "There's a LIB!" From that day forward, Eleanor became a believer in Lib's parking prayers.

Recently, one of Lib's daughters shared this journal entry.

> Friday, April 11
> Each day as I go to the bank for the deposit books, I say a believing prayer for a parking space. Once I said I wouldn't bother God for a place because I was NOT in a hurry—and there was no parking space. I don't want to bother God about little things but I really believe he is interested in everything.

As I write this story, I can only imagine Lib being ushered into heaven to her own parking sign that reads,

RESERVED FOR MY FAITHFUL SERVANT, LIB.
THE EFFECTUAL FERVENT PRAYER
OF A RIGHTEOUS [WOMAN] AVAILETH MUCH.
JAMES 5:16

A SWEET TEA SECRET
Believing and trusting God is something you can bank on.

page 210

Making It Big in a Small Southern Town

When I Moved to Edgefield County, there was one boutique owner who was quite the celebrity. Known for exhibiting excellent taste, hosting entertaining fashion shows, and creating fun games like *Bridal Bingo,* there is only one word to describe Mae: *amazing.*

Entering Mae's small boutique, you will be greeted by a Southern giant of fashion and flare. It all started in 1916 when the previous shop owner had boxes of women's clothing shipped by train from New York City to Batesburg, South Carolina. Just because you don't live in a Park Avenue penthouse doesn't mean you cannot dress like it.

Every year Johnston's Womens Club hosts an annual luncheon–fashion show fundraiser. The club members ask Mae to be the emcee and provide the wardrobe for the models. This is a much-anticipated event and Edgefield County's societal version of NYC's Fashion Week.

One year I was asked to run my sound system for Mae to emcee the show. As I was setting up, I watched Mae work her models. The first exercise was walking in an iambic pentameter rhythmic dance. The models lined up behind Mae as they wound their way around tables, walking and clapping in sync, adding confidence to their modeling skills. Most of the homegrown ladies, bless their hearts, needed help. But after Mae worked her magic, they could have signed with Wilhelmina Models.

The clothes sell out practically every time Mae emcees the fashion show. How does this happen? Well, Mae injects herself into each model, and with her beautiful Southern accent, it's a win-win. Mae uses verbiage like "Our model's outfit demands a simple clutch to enhance her hint of sparkle gracing her earlobes and guarantees that when she walks in her office Monday morning, she will be the new CEO . . . of her life. And who doesn't want to be the CEO of YOU?"

Need more proof of Mae's amazing abilities? Because of her fashion eye, Mae dresses some interesting women, including senators' wives, California media personalities, ballroom dancers, and a woman who won Best Dressed in Atlanta, along with countless other women across the country. Mae has not seen one of her most dedicated clients in ten years. This woman sends her chauffeur, along with a check, to pick up clothing. Mae never considers financial status when dressing women; her job is to create beauty in all of her clients.

I asked Mae the keys to her success. Here are some of my favorites:

- You must know the back door (business) before you can open the front door and sell.
- I stopped dressing brides when traditional Southern weddings changed; know your strengths.
- Never say, "I am tired" because the second time you will believe it.
- When advertising, use the "billboard" method—never use over seven words.
- The smallest efforts will help customers remember you tomorrow.
- Develop a "generational eye."
- Consultants don't sell; they dress.
- Your strength comes from your customers.

Did I mention that on her last birthday, Mae turned ninety? So what is the ultimate sweet tea success secret? Check out this amazing Mae quote. "I did not see myself as a woman. I am a businesswoman. When I considered my choices, the only option was to stop, and this was not an option."

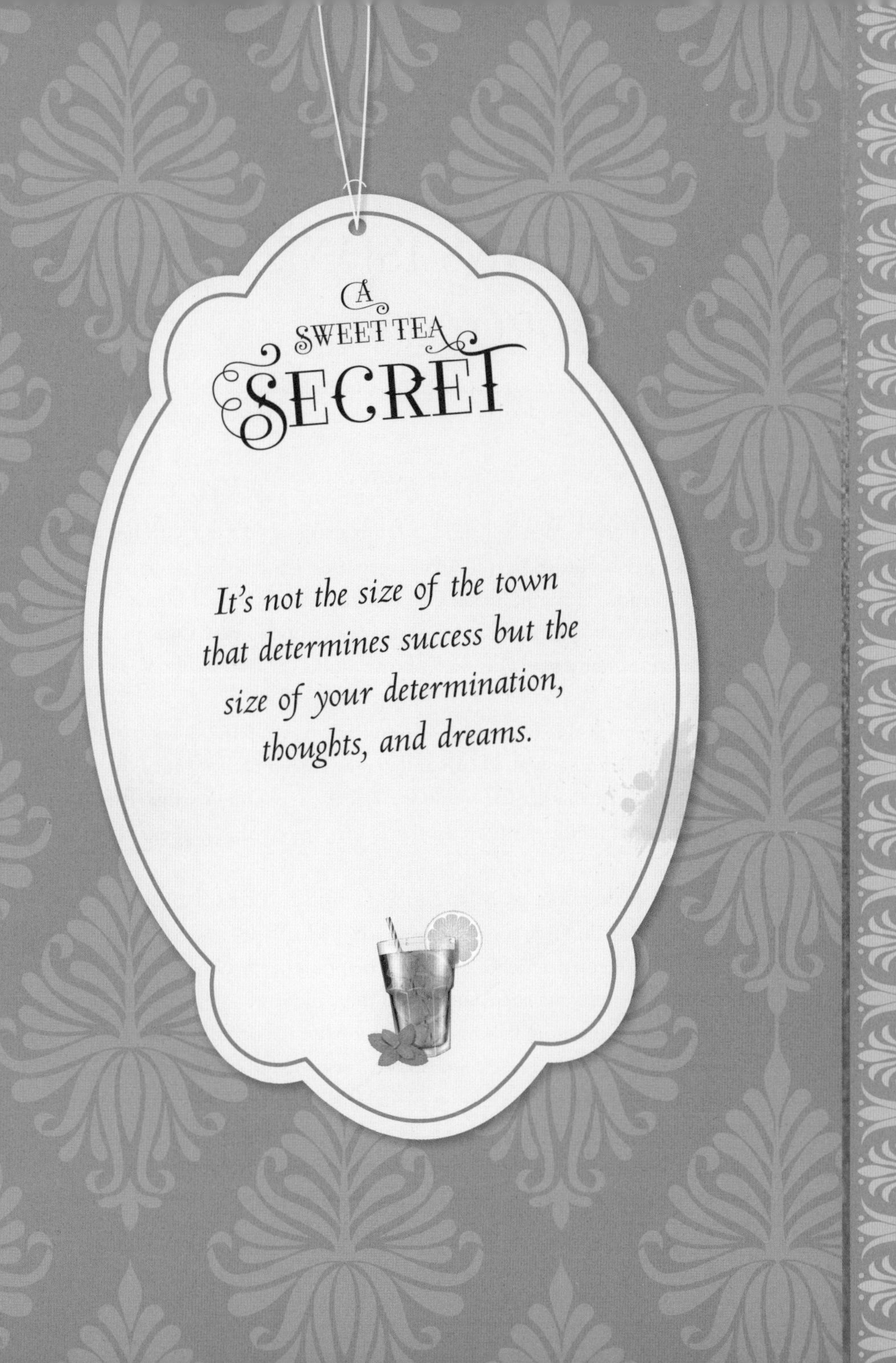
A SWEET TEA SECRET
It's not the size of the town that determines success but the size of your determination, thoughts, and dreams.

50
Johns Island Royalty

When I was a child, Momma would take me with her to visit her beautiful friend Ada. Every time I entered that amazing stucco home on the Bohicket River, I wanted to curtsy. I knew nothing about queens, kingdoms, or royalty but I knew I was in the presence of someone who was Johns Island's version of *Her Majesty, the Queen.*

Born with the distinguished Seabrook name, Miss Ada's family tree is far from being a wreath and can be traced back to 1666 with family land in excess of thousands of acres, according to a twelfth generational family member. In the South, we say this is some "high cotton."

Mr. Henry, love of Miss Ada's life, stood six feet, four inches tall. Right by his side was Mummy, Mr. Henry's pet name for her . . . all five feet, two inches of Ada. Theirs was a romance that began when both were teenagers and lasted for a lifetime.

On one offshore fishing trip, I saw Miss Ada cast her line into the Gulf Stream and hook a monster. I watched in amazement as she reeled in her catch. Because of her petite frame, Mr. Henry was her human fight chair and kept his strong arms wrapped around her waist. Never once did she hand her fishing rod to Mr. Henry; she did her own fighting. That spirit served her well.

Even within royal families, sadness can be a visitor. It was for

Miss Ada. She weathered financial ruin, the loss of a beautiful estate, the deaths of her husband, both sons, and a grandson. Who could bear such enormous tragedy without anger, bitterness, and shaking a fist at heaven? Miss Ada. No one ever heard her speak one word of resentment or self-pity. I was awed by the way she endured a life of tragedy that probably would have beaten the joy out of anybody else.

I positioned this story at the end of *Sweet Tea Secrets* because Miss Ada is the consummate Southern woman who was clothed with both strength and beauty. She always dressed with impeccable taste and style. I remember her fun hats, with flip-flops to match, and adorable sundresses. Her makeup was subtle but perfect, and not a hair on her head was ever out of place. Miss Ada was not a perfect, porcelain prima donna; a sister to seven brothers, she was full of mischief.

I remember when all the women in their group of friends decided to play a joke on the men and steal my daddy's boat, the *Never-No*. It was an innocent joke since they were only drifting down to the next dock. But they left the ropes behind. Daddy said he heard their cries for help and saw petite Miss Ada acting as their rope with her arms around the dock post, her body suspended in midair, while the other women in the boat held on to her feet. They laughed about that experience for years.

On a beautiful Monday morning in December, in the historic Presbyterian church on Johns Island, I sat in the church loft ready to sing "Amazing Grace," a song Miss Ada requested. This was her resurrection day, a time of celebration and a reminder of how we should live our lives.

This book has journeyed to some interesting places that celebrate our Southern ways. But as the tides continue to ebb and flow while gentle breezes lift the Spanish moss, what keeps our island alive is the eternal message of the life and legacy of our Johns Island folks, like Miss Ada.

Wear your heavenly crown with amazing grace, Miss Ada. You lived it.

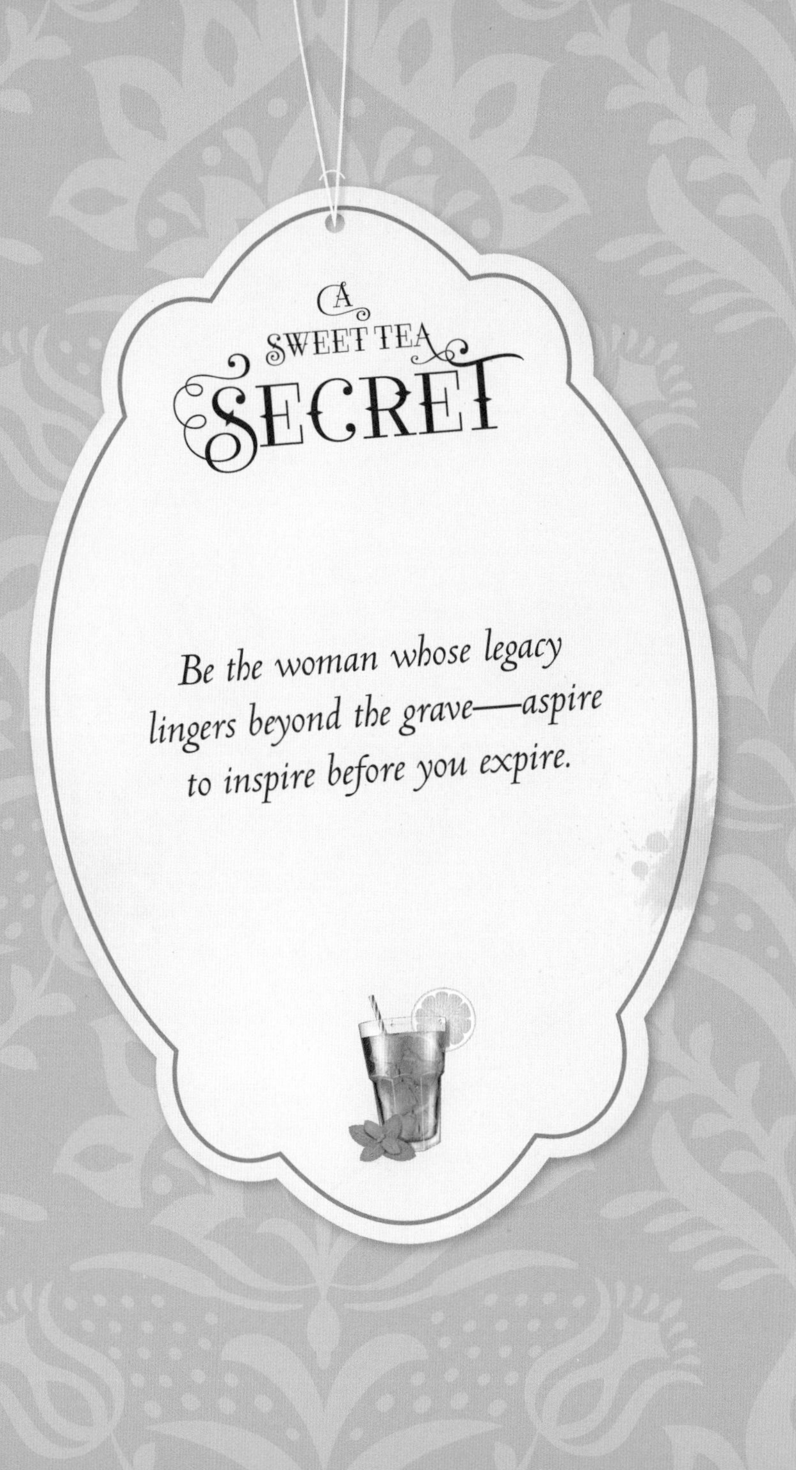
A SWEET TEA SECRET
Be the woman whose legacy
lingers beyond the grave—aspire
to inspire before you expire.

EPILOGUE

PLACES IN MY HEART

AS THE TIDES FLOW, change is inevitable.

While he was alive, every spring Daddy would very wisely take the jon boat down the creek to the Intracoastal Waterway on the flat low tide. He wanted to see how the ever-shifting tides had moved mounds of pluff mud, creating dangerous banks some call sandbars. Not knowing how to navigate what lies beneath can wreck the hull of a boat or keep you stranded for hours. In the Lowcountry we learn to live by the pull of the tides; we learn to be peaceful with the only thing that is consistent: change.

My South is so different now; it has evolved into a new South. Cultures are blending and our old Southern ways are challenged—admittedly in some ways for the better. But one thing that should never change is having pride in heritage since many who move to our Southland "ain't we people," as the Gullah expression goes.

Years ago when I was in college, my suitemate was a homesick Yankee from Minnesota. All of us "third floor gals" who lived in Asbury Hall on the Columbia College campus fell in love with Candi. My parents also loved Candi and her fun-loving parents, Don and Mikki Smith.

One weekend, Candi's family visited my family on our farm. Daddy went all out that weekend entertaining our new Minnesota friends. He took them for a long boat ride, then out to eat at our favorite seafood restaurant.

Finally, the ultimate Lowcountry, Southern experience—listening to LPs (long-playing recordings, for those who don't remember) featuring Southern comedian Jerry Clower and a recording of Lowcountry Gullah stories.

Don, Candi's dad, had a look of confusion on his face as he listened to the stories. But Mikki was laughing hysterically along with Daddy.

After the "show," Daddy commented to Mikki, "I am surprised that you could understand the Southern accents of Jerry Clower and all of the Gullah stories."

I will never forget Mikki's response.

"Oh, Ben, I could not understand a single word. I just wanted to be kind and laugh with you since you enjoyed it so much."

This story says it all to me. Y'all, thank you for laughing with us and enjoying our treasured sweet tea secrets from the deep-fried South. They touch the deepest parts of my heart, and I've loved sharing them with you. They represent memories from the past as they point toward the future.

The last scene in the movie *Places in the Heart* sums it up for me. All those in the movie who have lost their lives are back together, sharing Communion in an old country church at the height of the turbulent years of segregation and the Great Depression.

Heaven, to me, is a large Southern-style piazza with Pawleys Island Hammocks, Charleston rockers painted Charleston Green, and of course a giant joggling board. The porch ceiling would be painted "Haint Blue" to ward off evil spirits. Although our ocean along the Carolina coast is murky green, in my heaven an eternal breeze blows off a beautiful turquoise Atlantic Ocean. Gumpa and Lou tell stories as Thomas and our children, along with their spouses and children, lounge around. Momma, Daddy, Tootsie, my very fun sister, and my brother, who is living his best life, are by my side. Mama Jewell and Daddy Big John are there, too, and all the other Johns Island folks in our lives celebrate with us. Pets from long ago sprawl across the tongue-and-groove porch. Yellow jasmine curls around the columns, and spring daffodils cover the yard. A vine or two of kudzu may be visible, too, but only to remind us to be true to ourselves and our heritage as we all should.

Make no mistake, the main menu contains lots of love and laughter, served with endless helpings of sweet tea wisdom and Southern-fried humor. Side dishes of Charleston red rice, Gumpa's fresh *vege-tables* from his *guarden,* plus Tootsie's biscuits topped with a fresh slice of Daddy's tomatoes lie on the banquet table. Our Savior, Jesus, is seated in the center just like he should be living in the center of our lives on earth.

Right in front of that old Southern porch, a carriage tour stops, and the guide speaks with a Southern accent thicker than a pot of leftover grits.

So here is the last of the sweet tea secrets: *These sips and tips from my Southern upbringing are not secrets at all.* Regardless of "from whence you came," these are principles that will help you tap into your best self. They are not exclusive to the South. (I imagine you already figured that out.)

If you choose to embrace the lessons from each Southern tale, your life will be overflowing with servings of wisdom. Now add a full plate of humor, and your life will become a delicious eternal feast.

Acknowledgments

I am grateful to my parents, who left me with a sense of humor, taught me the importance of hard work, and encouraged me to always do the right thing. My moral compass, Thomas, has been a source of strength and a beacon of godly wisdom. My children are such a blessing. Holmes is hilarious and a constant source for new material. My sweet Caroline has matured into a Proverbs 31 woman; what a gift she is to our family!

Thinking back on my entire writing career, I have to start by thanking Dr. Broome, my college English professor, for giving me an F in writing. Big shout-out to Eddie Jones, who is the best guy ever to help authors write and promote books. Southern hugs to my first agent, Les Stobbe, for his wisdom and influence and for paving the way for me to work with Bob Hostetler. Bob introduced me to the wonderful folks at Tyndale House Publishers. I am blessed!

Notes

page xi **"the vine that ate the South":** "Kudzu," WebMD, accessed May 12 2020, https://www.webmd.com/vitamins/ai/ingredientmono-750/kudzu.

page xii **the tight grip of pluff mud:** Buff Ross, "Pluff Mud," *Charleston* magazine, February 2014, https://charlestonmag.com/features/pluff_mud_0.

page 1 **Has a pitcher of sweet tea at the ready:** Magnolia Lane makes and sells this plaque. See https://www.amazon.com/Magnolia-Lane-Southern-Wooden-Plaque/dp/B00TA46ZQU.

page 15 ***The Help*:** Directed by Tate Taylor, featuring Viola Davis, Octavia Spencer, and Emma Stone (DreamWorks, 2011).

page 18 **rabbit tobacco:** See Darryl Patton, "Rabbit Tobacco," The Southern Herbalist & Stalking the Wild, https://thesouthernherbalist.com/articles/rabbit_tobacco.html.

page 74 ***Sweet Home Alabama*:** Directed by Andy Tennant, featuring Reese Witherspoon, Patrick Dempsey, and Josh Lucas (Buena Vista Pictures, 2002).

page 88 **"It's not the size of the dog":** This quote is usually attributed to Mark Twain but cannot be traced to any of his books, letters, or speeches.

page 90 ***Fried Green Tomatoes*:** Directed by Jon Avnet, featuring Kathy Bates, Jessica Tandy, Mary Stuart Masterson (Universal Studios, 1991).

page 114 ***Sugar and spice and all things nice*:** Fred Nightingale, lyrics, BMG Rights Management US, LLC, EMI Music Publishing, Sony ATV Music PUB LLC. Lyrics licensed and provided by LyricFind.

page 154 ***Driving Miss Daisy*:** Directed by Bruce Beresford, featuring Morgan Freeman, Jessica Tandy, and Dan Aykroyd (Warner Bros. Pictures, 1989).

page 160 **"Dropkick me, Jesus, through the goalposts of life":** Lyrics by Paul Charles Craft, copyright 1976, Sony/ATV Music Publishing LLC, https://www.songfacts.com/facts/bobby-bare/drop-kick-me-jesus-through-the-goalposts-of-life.

page 220 ***Places in the Heart*:** Directed by Robert Benton, featuring Sally Field, Lindsay Crouse, and Ed Harris (TriStar Pictures, 1984).

About the Author

Jane Jenkins Herlong says of herself that *she is so Southern, she is even left-handed.* Born and bred on rural Johns Island, South Carolina, Jane traveled from the rows of her daddy's tomato field to the runway of the Miss America Pageant and beyond. A member of the Speaker Hall of Fame, Jane is a Southern humorist whose comedy is heard on SiriusXM radio. She travels throughout the country sharing her *sweet tea wisdom and Southern-fried humor* and is the author of five books. Jane is the wife of Thomas Herlong and mother of two children. The Herlongs live on the family peach farm in Harmony Community of Edgefield County.